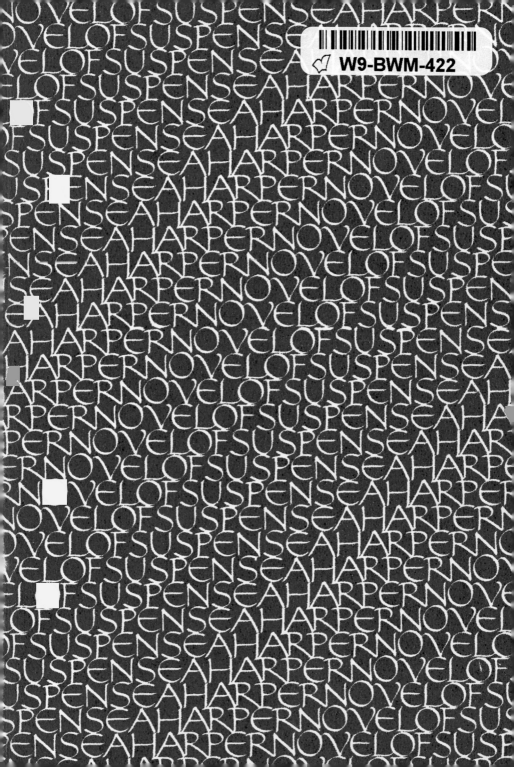

THE NIGHT OF
THE TWELFTH

A JOAN KAHN BOOK

BOOKS BY MICHAEL GILBERT

THE NIGHT OF THE TWELFTH

Michael Gilbert

HARPER & ROW, PUBLISHERS

New York, Hagerstown, San Francisco, London

A HARPER NOVEL OF SUSPENSE

FIRST U.S. EDITION

Library of Congress Cataloging in Publication Data

Gilbert, Michael Francis, 1912–
    The night of the twelfth.
    I. Title.
PZ3.G37367Ng3   [PR6013.I3335]   823'.9'14   75–30351
ISBN 0–06–011534–3

76 77 78 79 10 9 8 7 6 5 4 3 2 1

THE NIGHT OF
THE TWELFTH

A JOAN KAHN BOOK

1

"Virtually, then," said Constable Parks, "all you know is that Ted went out about two o'clock and hasn't come home."

He didn't say it unkindly. He had children of his own, and he knew exactly how Mrs. Lister was feeling.

"I didn't worry, not at first. He's ten, and big for his age. He's often out by himself. But when it got dark . . ."

That was the dividing line. While it was still daylight, though the child might be late there were a lot of reasons for delay. But when it got dark these comfortable arguments were no longer convincing. The black moment had come and you had to face it.

"I'll use your telephone," said Parks, "and have a word with Petersfield. Quicker that way."

He said, "I'm speaking from No. 6 Averley Road, Haydock Wood, Sergeant. The householder is Mrs. Lister. Her boy's gone missing. Name of Ted. Aged about ten—" Mrs. Lister said something. "Nearly eleven. Wearing a green school blazer with a red lion's-head crest, corduroy trousers, gray socks and gym shoes. No cap. Light hair. He went out to watch a cricket match at Tolhurst Green. He hadn't a bicycle. He was on foot. Normally he'd always be home for his tea at six. What I was going to do, I was going to see if I could find one or two of the people who were playing in the match. See if they noticed the boy."

To Mrs. Lister he said, "Don't you worry. We'll find him for you."

As he said it he realized that it wasn't very sensible to say "Don't worry," but what else could you say?

Des Maybury's plans for seducing Rosie Moritz were going ahead smoothly. The early part of the evening had been spent at No. 2 Jubilee Cottages, where Rosie's mother lived with her husband's father, old Mr. Moritz. Des and Rosie had the sort of appetites appropriate to a boy of nineteen and a girl of sixteen and they had done justice to a good meal. Then they had watched television. After that came the suggestion of a walk down to the Three Horseshoes in the village.

At this point Rosie's eyes had flickered toward her mother, but she had got the green light, and they had set out together companionably, arm in arm. It was a lovely evening in early June and just beginning to get dusk. On the stretch of dusty road that separated Jubilee Cottages from Brading village a few cars had bowled past them, but all their thoughts were on each other.

When they got to the Three Horseshoes, Des was provoked to find that Rosie's grandfather was still there. He was eighty, was nearly deaf, and walked very slowly with the aid of a rubber-tipped stick. He should have been on his way back to Jubilee Cottages by now. It was over half a mile and would take him half an hour. And there he was, stuck down in the corner, with a full pint in front of him, nattering to one of his cronies. Stupid old bugger. Of course he spotted them as soon as they came in. He might be deaf, but there was nothing wrong with his eyes.

Des ordered a lager and lime juice for Rosie and a pint of bitter for himself, and took the drinks into the corner farthest away from the old man. The room filled up steadily. Des stuck to beer, but managed to switch Rosie onto gin and lime.

At ten o'clock Mr. Moritz rose to his feet, said good night to the landlord, winked at Des and pottered out into the night.

"Good riddance," said Rosie. "He was counting every drink I had. It'll all go straight back to Mum."

"Might be run over by a car before he gets there," said Des

hopefully. "There was a girl knocked off her bicycle only last month."

"You're awful."

"Time for one more."

"I don't think I ought," said Rosie. "I shan't be able to walk home."

"I'll carry you," said Des. He pushed his way to the bar and bought the drinks.

At Petersfield Police Station, Superintendent Joliffe was organizing the hunt. He knew that when children went missing, speed was the important thing. Members of the Tolhurst Green cricket eleven had already been contacted. One or two of them had noticed a boy in a green blazer, and one, who knew him slightly, had spoken to him. This was in the early part of the afternoon, when their side were batting. When they went out to field, after tea, they had somewhat naturally lost sight of him. This meant looking up the visiting team, from Castle Hanbury. It was eleven o'clock by now, and some of them were in bed. When they realized what was wanted, they collected their scattered wits and tried to help. It was from one of them, the wicket keeper of the Castle Hanbury team, that they got their first hard news. He remembered a boy in a green blazer who had asked him the time. When he was told that it was six o'clock, he had departed hurriedly. "Late for his tea, I guess," said the wicket keeper.

This suggested two lines of investigation. First, a house-to-house inquiry along the road outside the cricket ground, to see if anyone had noticed the boy. "If he was in a hurry," said Joliffe, "ten to one he'd try to pick up a lift as quickly as possible." The second line was to beat through the fields and hedges between Tolhurst Green and Haydock Wood. It was two miles of open country, but Constable Parks had very sensibly got hold of a pair of shoes and stockings that Ted had been wearing the day before and dogs had been brought over from the police kennels at

Chichester. Most of the Tolhurst Green cricket side had involved themselves in the search as well.

It was ten to eleven when Des and Rosie left the Three Horseshoes. The night, viewed through a filter of alcohol, was more beautiful than ever. Des's arm was round Rosie's waist. She was laughing.

"What's the joke?" said Des.

"It seemed funny, being three."

"Three what?"

"Three horseshoes. Poor old horse. What did they put on his fourth leg?"

"Maybe he was a three-legged horse."

This was such a good joke that they stopped to laugh at it. As they went on again, Des's arm had slid smoothly upward, and his hand was now cupping Rosie's right breast. He could feel her excitement.

The lights of a car swung up behind them, and they crowded together on the verge as it went past.

"Look, Rosie," said Des. He sounded breathless. "There's something I want to say to you. We can't talk here. We'll be run over. Let's go down here for a moment."

It was a cart track. There was a gate at the end of it. As they climbed it he put his hands round the girl to help her down. His hands went under the sweater she was wearing and he felt the warmth of her bare skin. He was sure she was not going to say no.

It was a field of half-grown corn with a rutted track running along the hedgerow and dipping to the stream at the bottom. Des knew it well. He had driven one of farmer Laycock's tractors along it two days before and had noted it as a useful spot, accessible, but well hidden from the road.

He said, "Let's sit down for a bit."

"Old Laycock wouldn't half create if he saw us," said Rosie. "Squashing his corn."

They were lying down now, facing each other, and Des started on the next vital step. Holding Rosie gently round the shoulders with his left arm, he slid his right hand up under her sweater and started to unbutton her blouse.

She said, "I thought you had something you wanted to talk about," but she didn't stop him. He got his hand round behind her and unhooked the brassiere. Rosie said, "You ought to have brought a rug or something. This ground's bloody hard." She was calmer than he was, but not as calm as she was pretending to be.

The boy was lying half on top of her now, pressing his mouth down on hers, his hands busy on her body, which was trembling. The girl had abandoned pretense and was as hot as he was. In one of the movements they made together she flung her right arm out wildly.

And screamed.

Des said, "What the hell?"

She said, "Stop it. Stop it."

Des said, "Don't be bloody silly. You want it as much as I do."

"It's not you. It's something else. Something I felt. Put your hand . . . near mine. I'm not going to touch it again."

Cursing to himself, Des stretched out his left hand. It touched something cold. It was a naked human foot.

The five stations of the Surrey County Constabulary in the Horsham area took it in turns to do night duty. There were arrangements at the other four stations for emergency calls, but only the duty station was actually manned, normally by a sergeant and a constable.

On the night of June 12, Sergeant Callaghan was in charge. Callaghan was large and experienced, getting on toward retirement and inclined to be lazy. He found night duty particularly irksome. It spanned the hours between ten at night and six in the morning, and fell to his lot once a month. With him on this occasion was Constable Airey, young enough to be his son and inclined to be cocky.

At ten forty-five a message came through on the teletype. It was from the Hampshire Constabulary at Petersfield, and it reported that Edward Lister, aged ten, had been missing from his home at Haydock Wood since six o'clock that evening. A full description followed. The message was marked: "For information to other County Forces." Callaghan filed it.

At eleven-twenty there was a diversion. Two youths—who had been drinking all evening, had refused to leave when ordered to do so by the publican and had then become disorderly—were brought in. Callaghan booked the necessary particulars, escorted them to the cells and left them to sleep it off. He envied them. The hands of the clock seemed to have stopped.

At ten minutes to midnight the telephone rang. It was Constable Toft, from Brading. He reported, in carefully unemotional tones, that a boy had been discovered in a field, about eight hundred yards to the east of Brading village, on the secondary road from Horsham to Tilgates. The boy was partially undressed. His hands had been tied behind his back, and there was evidence that he had been assaulted and then strangled. Toft had ascertained that the boy was dead, but had not disturbed the body.

Callaghan wrote it all down, in laborious longhand, told Toft to stand by at Brading Station for further orders, and considered his next move.

Quite clearly the old man must be informed. He dialed Superintendent Oldham's home number and, after some delay, was answered by a sleepy female voice, which said that dad had gone up to town with mum and ought to be back at any moment.

Callaghan said, "Tell him to ring the station as soon as he does get back. It's urgent."

Miss Oldham said, between yawns, that she would leave a note on his pillow, and rang off.

What next?

After some consideration the sergeant rang Petersfield Police Station. He was put through to Superintendent Joliffe. The superintendent said, "Yes. That sounds like the boy. We've already got a lot of information about his earlier movements. I'll come round myself. Who's in charge at your end?"

Callaghan nearly said, "I am," but discretion stopped him. He said, "It'll be Superintendent Oldham, sir. The rendezvous is Brading Police Station. There'll be someone there to show you the spot."

At ten minutes past twelve the telephone rang again. This time it was Superintendent Oldham. Callaghan had got less than half-way through what he had to tell him when the superintendent cut him short. He said, "Operation Huntsman. Take all routine steps. You will act as communications center. I am going to Brading. Rendezvous Brading Police Station. First priority, contact the pathologist at Lewes General Hospital. Tell him to meet me at Brading."

Callaghan sat for a few moments staring sourly at the telephone. Operation Huntsman! Communications center! They might be in the bloody army. Who did the old man think he was? Bloody General Montgomery? He could ring Lewes. All right. But after that, what did he expect him to *do*, for God's sake? A thought occurred to him. There was one step he could take. He went to the door and bellowed. Constable Airey appeared at the double and stood awaiting orders.

"There's a bit of a flap on," said the sergeant. "What you'd better do is put the kettle on and make us both a nice cup of tea."

Superintendent Oldham reached Brading Police Station at one o'clock and found his opposite number from Petersfield already there. He listened to what Toft had to say, and drove back with him, stopping his car twenty yards short of the cart track. He placed one of his men at the mouth of the track and then drove back to the police station.

For the moment, there was nothing more that he could do. The orders in cases of this sort were explicit. This was the third case in the last twelve months of a child being kidnapped and as-saulted. All the cases had occurred in the home counties south of London. The county forces of Kent, Sussex, Surrey and Hampshire had set up a regional squad, based in London, to coordinate the search. Oldham had given the code word "Huntsman" at ten past twelve. The regional squad should be on the spot within a very short space of time. Until they arrived, the scene of the crime was to be sealed off but left undisturbed. In the previous cases enthusiastic but unskilled investigation had obliterated a lot of possibly valuable evidence.

The pathologist arrived at two o'clock and sat quietly with the two superintendents in the small room on the ground floor of Constable Toft's house that was Brading Police Station.

At three o'clock Oldham began to fidget. At three-fifteen he spoke to Horsham Police Station. Could Sergeant Callaghan again contact the regional squad and find out what the hell they were playing at.

Sergeant Callaghan's blank reception of this message told him the truth.

He said, "Then do it now," and rang off.

"Bit of a hitch?" said Joliffe.

"You might call it that," said Oldham grimly. "I'm afraid we shall have to wait. Do you think you could raise us a cup of tea, Toft?"

Toft thought that his wife would be able to do that.

It was ten past four, and the light was coming back into the sky, when two dark-gray saloon cars drew up outside Brading Police Station and Detective Chief Superintendent Jock Anderson stepped out of the front one.

2

Jock Anderson was thirty-five but might equally well have been ten years younger or ten years older. He had the pale, ageless face that is bred in the manses of the Scots and nurtured in their granite universities. The single disorderly feature in his disciplined appearance was a tuft of hair which rose like a cock's comb from the middle of his forehead.

He was standing at the mouth of the track in the full light of dawn. Fifty yards down the road, four cars were parked nose to tail.

He said, "It's up here, is it?"

"That's right, sir," said Toft. "You go over the gate at the end, turn right a piece, then left. The boy's two or three yards in, in the corn."

Anderson said, "How many people have been up to the body?"

"There's the couple who found it. And me."

"How did you go?"

"I kept clear of the track, on the left-hand side. And I didn't go round. I walked straight across through the corn. I thought it safer not to go round the outside of the field at all."

"Good. We'll make that the agreed track for anyone approaching the body. Up the left-hand side of the track. We'll have the gate wide open, I think. Then straight across the corner of the field to a point *behind* the body. Over to you, Doctor."

Dr. Rainey picked up his bag and departed, keeping carefully to the appointed line.

"Are those the boots you were wearing, Constable?"

Toft grinned and said, "I'm afraid they're my only pair, sir. The others are away being mended."

"We'll have to borrow them off you. You can wear slippers for half an hour." He turned to his second in command. "Now, is there anything I can do for you, David?"

Detective Inspector Rew, nearly six foot four and broad in proportion, said, "I've got the search-and-stop procedures started. Superintendent Oldham is coordinating that with the superintendent from Petersfield. If you've nothing more for me here, I'd like to get back to Horsham."

"Off you go. Sergeant, I want to block off the section of the road at the mouth of the track. We can't stop traffic, but you can put work-in-progress signs round the half section on this side. Then cover the area of the gate with plastic sheets. As soon as the doctor's finished, and you've done your stuff with your camera, Carter, we'll take the body out, sticking to the authorized route. Then I'll have the whole of that corner of the field covered, including the hedgerows at the angle. Nobody is to set foot in that area until the sheets are down. The doctor will be a fair time yet. I'll go back to the car."

Des Maybury was sitting in the back of Jock Anderson's car. Reaction had set in. He looked white and miserable.

"I'll have a word with the girl now," said Anderson. "Will you show me where she lives?"

"She won't be able to tell you nothing I haven't," said Des. "I don't think she's in any state to talk. She was carrying on so."

"We'll have to take a chance on that. It's those cottages up there, isn't it? No need to take the car. It'll do you good to stretch your legs."

Mrs. Moritz was waiting for them. It was clear that she had not been to bed. She said, "I gave Rosie a sleeping pill. It's the pills we have for grandfather, when he has one of his turns. I don't think we can wake her up."

"I'm sorry, but we shall have to try. How long has she been asleep?"

"I had her in bed just after midnight."

"Five hours," said Anderson. "That should be enough." He stopped, and said in quite a different tone of voice, "Midnight. Are you sure?"

Des said, "It would have been about then. We found the boy around a quarter to eleven. It took time to get hold of the constable. I had to take Rosie back first, see. She wouldn't be left alone. She was crying and carrying on."

"I'm not blaming you, son. I was just trying to work out these times. There's something that doesn't quite add up. But that's a problem for me, not you. Now, Mrs. Moritz, if you don't mind . . ."

"I'll do what I can."

When Rosic came down she was wide awake and quite composed. Most of her hysteria had been automatic cover against questions about what she had been doing in the field, and she was glad to note that the policeman seemed uninterested in her reason for going there. There was a look in her mother's eye which suggested that she might be going to raise the question later.

Times and places were what interested Anderson. He made a few notes. Her story seemed to tally well enough with what Maybury had told him. He could not be sure until he got the pathologist's report, but if other customers at the Three Horseshoes confirmed their time of leaving, it was impossible for them to have had any hand in the boy's death.

It had never seemed very likely, but in an inquiry of this sort all lines had to be ruled off neatly.

He said, "I'll have to borrow the shoes you were wearing. You can have them back as soon as we've made a plaster cast. And a list and description of the clothes you had on last night."

"The clothes?"

"That's right. You may not know it, but whenever you go anywhere you leave some trace behind. A fiber of wool. A scrap of fabric. We shall be going over the ground inch by inch. If we do find anything, it'll be important to know if it was left behind by you—or someone else."

"I see," said Rosie faintly. It did not seem to her that after so minute an examination the police could be in any doubt as to what she had been up to. It wasn't a crime, was it?

"I'd like a note of your blood group, too."

Rosie had no idea what her blood group was, but gave him the name of her doctor.

Anderson left Detective Fraser behind to collect the necessary details and was on the point of going when Mrs. Moritz said, "Do you think Grandfather might have seen anything? He was down at the Horseshoes. He left early. It takes him half an hour to get home. It's his knees."

"That's a very sound suggestion, Mrs. Moritz. Do you happen to know what time he started home?"

"Ten o'clock. Dead on," said Rosie.

"That's right," said her mother. "He got here a little past half past. The news had finished when he came in."

"Then I shall certainly have to have a word with him."

"Wake him up, you mean?"

"I'm afraid so."

"He won't be best pleased," said Mrs. Moritz. "But if you say so."

It took ten minutes to wake old Mr. Moritz up and explain what was wanted and fifteen to get him dressed and downstairs. After that there was a further delay because his teeth had been forgotten. Anderson waited patiently. When the information arrived it was well worth the wait.

"You saw a car coming out?"

"Out of that path leading up to Laycock's hayfield, Dad."

"Ah."

"You're sure it was that one?"

"That's right. Laycock's hayfield. Hadn't no lights on. That's not right, you know. Might have hit me."

"The car hadn't got any lights on."

"That's what I said." A further thought occurred to the old man. "Turned the lights on when he was driving away." There was something else that he was trying to remember. Something about the car and its lights. Anderson waited patiently. He never hurried a willing witness. But the memory had gone.

"Which way did it turn?"

"Turned right. Back to the village."

"Could you describe the car?"

The old man blinked, and made an indeterminate gesture with his hands. "Sort of middle size. Sort of ordinary car. Dark color. I couldn't really see."

"Did you happen to see the driver?"

"It was a man. I didn't see him very clearly at all. Tell the truth, I was busy wondering if it was going to hit me. Bursting out like that. No lights on."

"If you do think of anything else, let your daughter know, and she'll get in touch with me. I shall be at Haydock Wood, Mrs. Moritz. That's where the boy came from. I'll let you have the number to ring as soon as I know what it is."

"How anyone could do a thing like that to a boy," said Mrs. Moritz.

When Anderson got to Haydock Wood he found that Inspector Rew had been busy. An empty building, once a British Legion club, had been taken over and the Post Office was already busy installing telephones. Tables and chairs had been borrowed from the village hall. In the corner a portable printing machine was turning out the first of a series of notices, hundreds of which would be handed out and exhibited that day.

"Sorry I couldn't do better with the car," said Anderson. "If it had been a smart boy of ten who saw it—instead of an old man of eighty—he'd have given us the make, year, color and registration number."

"Lucky anyone noticed it," said Rew. He was busy pinning sections of the large-scale Ordnance Survey map to a square of hardboard propped against the wall. "How do you see this one?"

"Let's make some assumptions, shall we? When a man like this goes out on the prowl and picks up a victim, he doesn't turn back towards home with him. Whatever's going to happen, he wants it to happen as far away from his base as possible. He picked up the boy here. In Haydock Wood. He took him to Brading, which is due east. That meant he had to cross the A-24 somewhere. He wouldn't risk going through Horsham. He'd have used one of these side roads. And that means that when he turned right out of the track, he was starting out in the wrong direction. Again, quite a natural thing to do."

"Particularly if he saw the old man watching him."

"Right. But he'd want to get back onto the return route as soon as possible." Anderson stared at the map, with his eyes half closed, turning the lines on it into roads, thinking himself into the mind of a man who had committed a bestial crime, with the heat out of him, with one desire: to slink home unobserved.

"It would be the first turning to the right," he said at last. "That crossroads there. Then southwest through St. Leonards Forest, recrossing the A-24 there. After that there are too many choices. We'll net the whole of that area."

"Timings?"

"He'd have passed through that area between half-past ten and eleven."

Rew started to write this down and then stopped.

He said, "Are you sure . . . ?"

"All right," said Anderson. "I had noticed it. I'm going to deal with it now. You get on with your job."

At Horsham Police Station Anderson faced Superintendent Oldham. He said, "I've started the operation. It'll be slow work now. I shall need a lot of help."

"The chief constable is calling a conference at eleven. Any assistance you need, be sure you'll get it."

Anderson said, "Thank you." There was something more to be said, and both men knew it. There was no point in evading the issue. "What are you doing about Sergeant Callaghan?"

Oldham said, "I haven't decided yet."

"There'll have to be a disciplinary charge."

Oldham looked up sharply and said, "That's for the chief constable."

"He has no choice in the matter."

There was a long silence. Oldham was about to break it when Anderson forestalled him. He said, "I've spoken to the pathologist. When that man had the boy to himself, in the field, he took off all his clothes, except his shirt, and tortured him. There are burns from a cigarette lighter, the pathologist thinks, on his stomach and legs. The boy couldn't scream. A pad of foam rubber had been forced into his mouth and taped there. Then he killed him, but not too quickly. The pathologist thinks that the cord round his neck was tightened and loosened again more than once. The marks of the boy's teeth where he bit his tongue in his agony are clear in more than one place."

Anderson had been speaking quietly and with a total lack of emphasis, which seemed to make the words he was speaking more horrible.

"It is possible—not certain, by any means, but possible—that the sort of precautions we took at half-past three, when we finally got your message, if we had taken them before midnight—which we could have done if Callaghan had given the signal himself—might have enabled us to catch this man before he got home. Even if we hadn't headed him off, people's recollections would have been fresher, the chances of picking up the trail far stronger. A slip-up like that puts the next boy in danger. It mustn't happen again. That's why an example must be made of Callaghan."

Oldham said, "I see." It was neither acceptance nor refusal.

Anderson got up and stretched himself. He said, "The man's gone to earth. He's hidden himself away somewhere and thinks he's safe. But I'm going to dig him out and nail his hide up on the wall. No matter what it costs. No matter how long it takes. That's a promise."

3

"Gentlemen," said Mr. Fairfax, "I welcome you back and hope that you enjoyed the brief respite from your labors."

"Too brief," said Arthur Diplock.

"But very welcome," said Constance Latrobe.

"You will be glad to know that as a result of strenuous efforts by the gardening staff and Sergeant Baker, we have, I think, got rid of the last of the unwelcome visitors introduced by Palel Major."

"Scoured the ship, eh, Headmaster?" said Commander Gaze.

"We did indeed. On Saturday, after you left, we sealed up all the windows in the classrooms, changing rooms, lavatories, bathrooms and dormitories. The sanitary authorities, having told us they would be here in the early afternoon, naturally did not arrive until after tea. We therefore had to work until nine o'clock that night, but we succeeded in disinfesting every room the boys had used. Without Sergeant Baker, I don't think we should have done it. He was a tower of strength."

"Lovely to be able to stop scratching," said Latrobe.

"Mostly imagination," said Commander Gaze.

"I'm not sure," said Nigel Warr. "The first thing I did after lunch on Saturday was to get Elizabeth to wash my hair for me."

"To turn to pleasanter subjects," said Mr. Fairfax, "I have succeeded, once more through the good offices of Colonel Brabazon, who has been so kind to the school in so many ways, in getting a temporary replacement for Mr. Mollison. It was quite clear from his medical report that he would not be fit for the rest of the term. The doctor advised complete rest."

"One-B has much to answer for," said Warr.

"We shall therefore not have to rearrange the timetable, as we feared might be the case. The new man—his name, by the way, is Kenneth Manifold—will simply take over Mr. Mollison's classes. His special subjects seem to be French, history and English, so that fits in quite well. He can have Mr. Mollison's bedroom."

"Where's he going to keep his car?" said Mr. Diplock. "There's no room in the garage."

"How do we know he's got a car?"

"All assistant masters have cars these days. It was very different when I started teaching."

"In those far-off days," said Latrobe, "I suppose you all rode horses."

"I'm not quite as old as that, thank you."

"Set your minds at rest," said Warr. "No one will have to move out of the garage. He's got a motorbike."

All looked out of the window. A motor bicycle had turned in at the lodge gates and was coming up the front drive of Trenchard House School.

The headmaster said, "I think you're right. This must be he. Sit tight, gentlemen. I'll bring him straight in."

The four men relaxed slightly as the door shut behind him. Arthur Diplock got out his pipe and started to scratch out the blackened interior with an implement designed for extracting stones from horses' hoofs. Warr said, "Poor old Molly. I knew One-B were getting on his wick, but I didn't expect him to have a full-scale nervous breakdown."

"I warned him about his health," said the Commander. "What he needed was more exercise. I told him not to fug in the common room smoking cigarettes all day."

"I agree," said Latrobe. "There's nothing wrong with One-B.

They're very nice boys, taken individually. All they need is under-standing—"

"And beating twice a week," said Warr.

"In thirty years of schoolmastering—" began Mr. Diplock, but was cut short by the opening of the door. Four pairs of eyes studied the man who came in behind the headmaster. Reddish-brown hair, thick eyebrows, a nose that was not hooked, but had a curious hook at the end of it, like the beak of a raptor, a long chin, a head set on a thick neck. A suit that had once been good, but had been worn too long. Warr thought: He doesn't look like a man who suffers from nerves. One-B might be in for a lively time. Commander Gaze thought: Athletic type, run to seed a bit, but might help with the games. Diplock thought: Unusual sort of assistant master. Could have been sacked from some other job, I suppose, and come here in search of a soft billet. Latrobe thought: Looks a bit of a brute.

When Mr. Fairfax had completed the introductions, he said, "You'll have plenty of time to get to know each other later. I'll take Manifold off and show him round. I think the sergeant is about to ring the bell."

The tour finished in the headmaster's study. Mr. Fairfax said, "You've been reserving judgment, I can see. What do you think of it all?"

"It must have been a remarkably fine house. Before they started adding all those bits onto it."

Mr. Fairfax looked surprised, and said, "Built in 1775 by a nabob who came home from India with a fortune squeezed out of the natives and died of syphilis five years later."

"Poetic justice," said Manifold. "But I imagine what you really meant was, what do I make of you all. It's early in the day to say, of course, but I expect I shall get along all right."

"You've taught in preparatory schools before?"

"Didn't Colonel Brabazon give you the details?"

"It was all done in such a hurry that I didn't get anything in writing. He mentioned Broughton House. That was in Cheshire, wasn't it? It closed down unexpectedly at the end of last term."

"It wasn't unexpected," said Manifold. "At least, not by me. It had been going downhill for years. It was the drains that finished it off. Coupled with three cases of diphtheria."

"Had you much experience before that?"

"I helped my father run his school in Kenya. It was going very nicely until our new black masters took it over for peanuts and kicked us out."

"I see," said Mr. Fairfax. Manifold, with his obvious air of maturity and his very slightly run-down appearance, was beginning to make more sense to him. "You may find this an unusual school in some ways. I don't mean that it's a school for abnormal boys. As far as I know, they're all perfectly normal. But we do specialize in taking boys whose parents are abroad, in the services, or on business. One boy we have to keep a very special eye on is Jared Sacher."

"Is that Ben Sacher's son?"

"You know him?"

"Only what I've read in the papers. He's the Israeli ambassador in London, isn't he? The Arabs have already had two tries at killing him. He sounds a remarkable man."

"His son is a remarkable boy. There are others—Peter Joscelyne is one—who have no real home. His parents are separated and the mother lives abroad."

"What does he do in the holidays?"

"He sometimes spends them with one of his friends. He spent half term with the McMurtries. That's Alastair McMurtrie, our head boy. A very sound type. When they've nowhere else to go, the boys are very welcome here in the holidays."

"Friends for your own children."

"That would be so," said Mr. Fairfax shortly, "but in fact I have no children of my own." He took a list from his desk. "That's the roll of One-B. They'll be your main responsibility. They've got a bit out of hand lately. Your predecessor had a lot of educational theories, but not much common sense. I don't think you'll have any trouble with them. Keep an eye on Paine. He's the oldest and inclined to be the ringleader."

Manifold said that he would keep an eye on Paine.

"You'll be taking One-A for French. That's our scholarship form. Only seven boys, but a very good lot. McMurtrie, Sacher and Joscelyne I've mentioned. Roger and Billy Warlock. You wouldn't think they were twins to look at them. Their father's Peter Warlock, the actor. Terence Paxton. His father's a barrister. Who have I left out? Oh, yes. Monty Gedge. He's the fat boy. Every school seems to have one. It's nothing to do with what he eats. Paxton eats twice as much as Gedge and stays thin as a rake. Now—I expect you've got questions you'd like to ask me."

"Only one at the moment. What disciplinary powers do I possess?"

"A good question." Mr. Fairfax went again to his desk and took out two little booklets, composed of a number of tear-out pages, like small checkbooks. The printing in one book was in black, the other in red. He said, "We call these merits and demerits. The boys refer to them as blacks and reds. You award them for conduct which deserves them."

"And the awarding of a demerit is the only power of punishment that I possess?"

"No. Single boys or whole forms can be kept in and given extra work during the free hour, between five and six in the evening. Or in extreme cases, during the Saturday evening, when we normally have a film show."

"May I beat them?"

The directness of the question seemed to take Mr. Fairfax aback. He said, "In no circumstances whatsoever. No one is allowed to lay hands on a boy, except me."

"I just wanted to know," said Manifold easily.

"In serious cases you can award a double demerit. The boy will have to bring it to me and explain what happened. If I am not satisfied with his explanation, I will beat him. But I don't expect to have to do so more than once or twice a term." He added, "I am not as didactically opposed to corporal punishment as some modern educationalists seem to be, but I can assure you that I am fully aware of the dangers, both to the beater and the beaten."

Manifold inspected Form One-B with interest. With equal interest Form One-B inspected him. He took a piece of paper, a ruler and a pencil from the desk and divided the paper neatly into boxes, one representing each of the twelve desks in front of him. He then directed his attention to the large, spotty boy in the front left-hand desk and said, "Name?"

"Paine, sir."

"Yes, I thought you must be," said Manifold. He inscribed the name in the left-hand box and repeated the process until all twelve boxes were full. Then he said, "That is your form order —for the moment. Paine number one, Simmons number two, and so on, down to Shepherd, number twelve. Now—to work. History. The reigns of the Tudors. A fascinating period." He turned over the pages of the textbook in front of him. "How far had you got with Mr. Mollison?"

"It was about page eighty-three," said Simmons.

"It wasn't," said Paine. "We hadn't got to Elizabeth."

"Of course we had. Just because you were asleep—"

Manifold hit the desk hard with the flat of his hand. It made a slamming noise which echoed round the room. In the silence that followed he said, still pleasantly, "When I ask a question it will be answered only by the boy I happen to address. Understood, Paine?"

"Yes, sir."

"You're quite certain that you had finished with the reign of Bloody Mary."

"Yes, sir."

"Good. Then tell me the name of one of the bishops she burned at the stake."

Paine opened his mouth slightly, and then said, "I can't remember the exact names, sir."

"Simmons?"

"Cranmer."

"Right. Change places with Paine."

"Change places?"

"Certainly. Having answered the question correctly, you go up. Paine goes down. Jump to it." The last words came out with such a crack that Simmons shot out of his desk like a rabbit startled by the sudden report of a gun.

"I see that I must explain my system to you. We will have a question-and-answer session each period, based on the work done the period before. A wrong answer you go down, a right answer you go up. At the end of the week, the boy at the top gets a merit. The boy at the bottom gets a demerit. If the same boy is at the bottom two weeks running, he gets a double demerit. Three weeks, a treble demerit. Right? Another burnt bishop, Paine?"

"Er—"

"Hills?"

"Latimer, sir."

"Up Hills, down Paine."

By the end of the half hour that followed, Paine was sweating freely and was occupying the desk one from the bottom. Relieved as any boxer on the ropes to hear the bell, he gathered his books together and made thankfully for the door. Manifold said gently, "Sit down, Paine."

"But that was the bell, sir. We've got maths with Mr. Diplock next."

"The bell, Paine, is a notification to *me* that the period is over. Not a signal for a stampede. It seems to me that you need some practice in form-room deportment. You will all come here at five o'clock this evening, and we will see if we can manage things in a more orderly fashion. Goodbye for the moment."

"We shall have to double up some of the parts," said Latrobe. "Fourteen characters and only eight of us. Granville-Barker says that Shakespeare constructed the last scenes so that, at a pinch, the same boy could play Viola and Sebastian. It means cutting out the confrontation and juggling some of the exits and entrances."

"That looks like *two* parts for you, Peter," said Alastair McMurtrie. "Who have you got for me, Connie?"

"Sir Toby Belch, I think."

"Why do I always get the large, coarse comic characters?"

"Think it out," said Jared Sacher.

"Malvolio for you, Roger, and Maria for Billy."

This seemed natural casting since Roger was tall and serious, Billy was small, dark and cheerful.

"Terry, you can do Sir Andrew. Monty can be Feste *and* both sea captains. That is, if we don't cut out the first Sebastian scene altogether. The great advantage of doing Shakespeare is that most of the audience know the plot, so you don't have to do too much explaining."

"I suppose I'm Olivia," said Jared Sacher.

"You suppose correctly," said Latrobe, and blushed very slightly as he said it.

"Then who's going to be Orsino?"

"I thought I might take that part myself."

" 'If music be the food of love, play on,' " said Peter Joscelyne softly, and Billy kicked Roger Warlock on the ankle and got a return blow in the stomach.

"Less of that," said Latrobe sharply. "This is an English literature class, not a judo session."

"Is this thing definitely on, then?" said McMurtrie.

"All fixed. For the last Saturday of term. On the lawn if it's fine. In the gym if it's wet. So you've got just over five weeks to learn your parts. We can have a first run-through, reading lines, on Saturday, last period before lunch. Now we'd better get back to Chaucer."

Lucy Fairfax helped herself to a large glass of preluncheon sherry and said, "What's the new man like? I hope he's not a drip like Mollison."

"He's not a drip," said Mr. Fairfax.

"I caught a glimpse of him in first break. He looks reasonably virile." As she said this she gave her husband a sly glance out of the corner of her brown eyes. Her husband said, "I expect he is. Don't drink too much of that stuff or the boys will smell your breath."

"Once they get into the dining room," said Lucy, "they won't smell anything but cabbage. Cook has burnt it again."

"I hear you pulverized One-B," said Alastair McMurtrie.

Manifold inspected the seven boys who made up One-A. Most of them he could already identify. McMurtrie, freckled, snub-nosed, well-developed, with the build of a second-row forward. Jared Sacher, a dark beauty with alarmingly intelligent eyes. Peter Joscelyne, small, quiet and withdrawn. The Warlock twins, totally unlike each other, yet each with a suggestion of their father's often photographed face. The fat boy with the permanent smile must be Monty Gedge and that left—forgotten the name: father a barrister—Paxton. Terence Paxton.

"We had quite a lively first meeting," he agreed.

"I found Paine sitting in a corner after lunch mumbling dates to himself."

"They're a bunch of stupid kids," said Sacher. "It was only that Mr. Mollison was such an ass. I'm sorry, sir. But he was. You know what started the rot? It was in Scripture. One of them asked him what a harlot was. Well, really! That's been a standing joke for years. All he had to say was, 'It's the biblical name for a tart,' and they'd have known where they were."

"What *did* he say?"

"According to those that were present, he blushed and said, 'Well, Paine, it's—um—a girl who has—er—lost her way.' After that they pulled his leg until it nearly came off. When anyone on one of his walks took a wrong turning, they used to shout in unison, 'Come back, you harlots.'"

"Are you going to be very strict with us?" said Joscelyne. "You needn't be, you know. Actually, we do a lot of work."

"You do a lot of talking," said Manifold. "I've no objection to you talking, but as this is meant to be a French lesson, all conversation from now on will be in French. *Vous me donnerez, l'un après l'autre, une description exacte de ce que vous avez fait pendant le mi-trimêstre.*"

"*Quant à ça,*" said Sacher, "*si je vous rends un conte exacte, je jure que vous ne le croyerez point.*"

"That's just Sacher showing off," said McMurtrie. "His father takes him to France in the holidays. *Moi je passe les trois jours—*"

"*Passai.*"

"*Je passai les trois jours chez moi. J'ai mangé beaucoup.*"

"*Vous n'avez pas mangé beaucoup,*" said Joscelyne. "*Vous avez mangé trop. Et vous avez été—* What's the French for 'disgustingly sick'?"

"It's not bad beer," said Nigel Warr. "They do at least keep it in wooden barrels, not in metal cylinders."

"It's all right," said Manifold. "And I don't mind telling you I can do with it."

"You seem to have put the fear of God into One-B. If T.E.F. would let us beat them up occasionally, we'd have no trouble at all. In my humble opinion, six with a gym shoe is more effective than any number of paper demerits."

"On the other hand, I enjoyed One-A."

"Yes. They're a remarkable crowd. We haven't had a better scholarship form in the two and a half years I've been here. McMurtrie and Joscelyne have both got first-class brains, but Jared Sacher's a freak. To talk to him sometimes, you'd think he was a disillusioned middle-aged man."

"He's a raving beauty," said Manifold. "A lot of boys are attractive at that age, but only a Jewish boy could look quite like that."

Nigel looked at him curiously, and said, "Better not let Connie hear you talking like that. He looks on him as his private property."

"He's nobody's property, except his own. By the way, is this all right?"

"Is what all right?"

"Drinking here. The head doesn't mind?"

"Certainly he doesn't mind. Why should he?"

"They were rather fussy about it at my last place. If we wanted to drink we had to go a bit further away. Bad example."

"We can't be setting a bad example to the boys," said Nigel reasonably, "because they don't come here. At least, not as far as I know. Where was your last place?"

"Broughton House. Up in Cheshire. Drink up and I'll get you another."

Nigel watched him curiously as he made his way to the bar, ordered the drinks and carried them back. He said, "I hope you won't mind turning this into a threesome. With any luck, Elizabeth should be here soon."

"Is that the very attractive girl I saw helping Mrs. Fairfax dish out the cocoa?"

"That's her. Elizabeth Shaw. Assistant matron, assistant housekeeper, assistant wardrobe mistress and general dogsbody. A very nice kid."

"Are you . . . ?"

"That's right," said Nigel. "We are. But it's still unofficial. As long as it stays that way, Mrs. F. will tolerate it—just. If it became official I think we should both get the boot. And that would be awkward."

"You'd get a place somewhere else pretty quickly."

"It isn't as easy as all that. Elizabeth has to look after her stepfather, old Mr. Merriam. They've got a house in the village. We passed it on the way down from the school. He's completely paralyzed. Not a stroke. Something to do with the nerves in his spine. It came on gradually and couldn't be stopped."

"How horrible."

"He can't get out of his chair now without help. His sight and hearing are still all right, which is a blessing, because he can read and listen to the wireless. But he can hardly talk at all. Just grunts a bit. Elizabeth seems to understand it."

"If she has to look after him, how on earth does she manage to do her work at the school?"

26

"That's just it. Mrs. Loveday, who lives next door, copes with Mr. Merriam by day. She's glad to earn a bit of extra money doing it. Elizabeth puts him to rights in the morning and takes over when she gets back in the evening."

"A bit of luck finding a neighbor prepared to help."

"It certainly was. And that's what would make it so damned awkward if we had to move."

"Incidentally," said Manifold, trying to visualize what "putting him to rights" might involve, "I should have thought it took a bit of doing, looking after him single-handed."

"She's a wonderful girl," said Nigel. "But of course she couldn't do it if she hadn't had some early training as a nurse. They teach them to hump people around. I give a hand when I'm down there."

They were finishing their second drinks when Elizabeth arrived. She seemed to know most of the characters in the bar by their Christian names. Not a kid, thought Manifold. A competent young woman, in real age a good deal older than the agreeable but juvenile Nigel. Sexually extremely attractive. Not pretty. Her face was too strong for prettiness. It was the way she carried her beautiful body, as though she was fully aware of its potentiality, both as a magnet and as a weapon.

She said, "Well. And what are your reactions after one day of Trenchard House?"

"It's better than his last place," said Nigel. "They wouldn't let the masters drink at the local."

"Dotheboys Hall. Don't put too much tonic in. I've had a hard day and I need a slug of hard liquor."

"Mrs. F. being bloody again?"

"As per usual."

"I thought I saw you having a heart-to-heart after the boys' supper."

"You thought right. Holbrow Three, who's really too young to be at boarding school at all, spilled half his cocoa and I told him to get a cloth from the pantry and mop it up. At that moment"
—Elizabeth took a deep mouthful of her gin—"Mrs. F. surged up

and said, 'Really, the fees we extract from these poor little boys, we can't expect them to act as scullery maids as well. Just clean it up for him, would you, Elizabeth.' "

"The sweet creature," said Nigel.

"You'd better watch your step, Ken."

"Why me?" Manifold asked.

"Anything under forty in trousers is meat and drink to our Lucy. And there isn't all that much competition."

Manifold, running a mental rule over old Mr. Diplock, the bluff Commander Gregory Gaze and young Constance Latrobe was forced to agree that the candidates for the role of Lothario were thin on the ground.

It was after eleven when they left the pub. Nigel had stopped off at Elizabeth's cottage and Manifold walked the four hundred yards from Boxwood village to the school by himself. The grounds of Trenchard House occupied the angle between the secondary London-to-Chichester road and a side turning which took in Tinmans Common and Rudgwick Green and joined the main Chichester road a couple of miles lower down. Nigel had advised him to use the side gate on this road. There was a path from it directly to the north wing of the house, where most of the staff had their rooms.

"If you use the front door," he said, "you'll probably find Mrs. F. waiting for you with a rolling pin."

"Or an open invitation," said Elizabeth.

Manifold was grinning at the thought as he let himself in and made his way to what had formerly been Mr. Mollison's bedroom. He wondered about Mr. Mollison. The weapons in the hands of a preparatory school master are such that nobody, surely, needed to tolerate disorder. Perhaps he had been a masochist. Just as some men got a thrill out of being tyrannized by women, he supposed that some men might get a similar kick out of being bullied by small boys. It seemed improbable.

The bed was hard, but not uncomfortable. Manifold was turning over for the third time and on the brink of sleep when he heard the creak of a board in the passage outside.

Mrs. Fairfax? Hardly as quick off the mark as that, surely.

The door of the next room opened and shut. Commander Gaze, it seemed, had also been out late.

4

Once more, thought Commander Gaze, and he would have been round the cricket field six times. His face, normally brick red, was bright scarlet and his white hair was fluffed, but his breathing was unhurried and his heart seemed to be behaving properly. A lifetime in the Royal Navy taught you one thing at least. How to keep fit.

The pavilion. Two hundred yards to go. Commander Gaze had enjoyed the Royal Navy. The recollection of some of the indignities he had suffered as a midshipman still had the power to make him squirm, but after that it had mostly been simple pleasure. There had been a few bad moments during the war, of course.

Sixth round accomplished. Now for a cold bath. He hoped that the new man was not going to be difficult about sharing the bathroom.

The headmaster gazed down at the school assembled for morning prayers. The boys looked reasonably alert. Like Commander Gaze, they had performed the curious ritual of plunging their bodies into cold water, although in their case from compulsion rather than choice. The new man looked reasonably fresh. Latrobe seemed to be half asleep. Arthur Diplock was a disgraceful sight. He liked to win an extra five minutes in bed by shaving after breakfast. Warr had not yet arrived. He would try to sneak in unnoticed during the hymn.

"New every morning is the love
   Our wakening and uprising prove;
   Through sleep and darkness safely brought,
   Restored to life, and power, and thought.

"New mercies, each returning day,
   Hover around us while we pray;
   New perils past, new sins forgiven,
   New thoughts of God, new hopes of heaven."

Did the words mean anything to the boys who were singing them? Were they aware of the perils? He very much doubted it. Ah! Here came Nigel, trying to slide in unobtrusively.

The lesson was read by the boys in turn. Today it was McMurtrie. A very satisfactory boy, and an excellent head of the school. His father, Sir Charles McMurtrie, was something high up in one of the curious outfits which operated around Queen Anne's Gate. Alastair read like a veteran, casting his eyes ahead to sort out the awkward passages. No hesitation, no fumbling. He would go a long way.

"O Lord, our heavenly Father, Almighty and everlasting God, who hast safely brought us to the beginning of this day . . ."

Bring us safely to the end of it, thought Mr. Fairfax. He pronounced a blessing on his flock and watched them file in to breakfast.

"You will have to make arrangements to isolate Maxwell at once," said Mrs. Fairfax.

"Oh?" said Elizabeth. "Why?"

"Why? Because he's got measles, of course. Didn't you see his stomach?"

"I saw his stomach," agreed Elizabeth. "But it can't be measles. He hasn't been outside the school in the first six weeks of term. And if he'd picked it up at half term, it wouldn't have shown yet. Anyway, measles spots usually start on the chest and shoulders."

"If it isn't measles, what is it?"

"Heat rash. Probably brought on by overeating at half term."

"We can't take the risk."

"There's no risk involved," said Elizabeth. "Yes, Mr. Manifold?"

"I hope I'm not interrupting something important. I just wanted to find out about laundry arrangements."

"Laundry goes on Fridays and comes back on Tuesdays. There's a basket in the bathroom you share with the Commander. If there's some washing you want done urgently—"

"I can last out until Tuesday," said Manifold with a smile. He had enjoyed the conversation he had overheard. There was an unexpected touch of steel in Elizabeth. A nurse's training evidently taught you more than how to empty bedpans.

"Up, down. Up, down," said Sergeant Baker. "Throw those shoulders back, open the chest, breathe deeply. One, two. Now down and touch your toes. Gedge, you're bending your knees."

"I'm not the right shape for touching my toes," said Gedge.

"Then we must make you the right shape, mustn't we. That's what P.T. is all about."

"You're out of date, Sergeant," said Sacher. "It's not called physical training now. It's physical education. It's meant to be a gentle and rhythmic coordination of mind and body."

"Lovely," said Sergeant Baker. "We'll do a few gentle and rhythmic press-ups. On the front, down. Raise the body slowly, and lower it slowly, but do *not* allow it to touch the ground."

"I don't believe he's a qualified instructor at all," said Joscelyne. "He's just a sadist."

The staff room contained one very old armchair, two wicker chairs, one revolving chair with a dangerous tipback, and one deck chair. Mr. Diplock had prescriptive rights to the armchair. The others took pot luck. It was the eleven o'clock break.

"The tea's all right," said Nigel, "but I shouldn't try the biscuits, not unless you've got good teeth. Mrs. F. buys a jumbo-size tin at the beginning of term and tries to make it last for twelve weeks."

"No milk or sugar, thank you," said Commander Gaze. "Never touch them. Nor biscuits."

"What a sad life you lead," said Nigel. "I eat everything I like, and I never get any fatter. What did you do at half term, Dip?"

"I went up to London."

"For a weekend of lechery?"

"I am, alas, too old for lechery," said Mr. Diplock. "I went to stay with my aunts. They have a house in Barnet and keep a goat in the garden."

"What about you, Connie?"

"I went to Guildford. They've got a new theater. I wanted to have a look at it."

"If you went to Guildford on a summer weekend," said Manifold, "you were lucky to find a room in a hotel, I guess."

"As a matter of fact, I didn't. I slept in my car."

"You can't sleep in an Austin 1100," said Nigel. "Not unless you've got collapsible legs."

"Well, I didn't sleep much," agreed Latrobe. "But it was worth it. It's a beautiful theater, and it was *The Three Sisters.* Absolutely one of my favorite plays."

"Russian," said the Commander. "Long-haired introverts sitting round in a dark room talking psychological claptrap."

"Have you ever seen one of Chekhov's plays?"

"No, thank God."

"Then it's pretty stupid to criticize them."

"What did you do, G.G.?" asked Nigel hastily.

"I took a bit of God's fresh air into my lungs. Went for a hike along the South Down Ridgeway. Covered twenty miles. Spent the night in a pub, and walked home on Sunday."

"That sounds an excellent program," said Manifold. Disregarding Nigel's warning, he had sunk his teeth into a gingersnap and had some difficulty in proceeding. "Wha putch ayat?"

"I beg your pardon."

33

"I said, what pub did you stay at?"

"The White Horse at Tilgate. Why?"

"Good pubs are always worth remembering," said Manifold.

"I wouldn't walk twenty miles to get a drink," said Mr. Diplock.
"However good it was."

The discussion was broken up by the bell.

"Are you coming down to the Lion?" asked Nigel.

"Not tonight," said Manifold. "I've decided to be a conscientious schoolmaster every other night. A history test for One-B
and a bit of French translation to get ready for One-A. Linguists
like Sacher and Joscelyne keep you up to the mark."

He had worked steadily for half an hour when Mr. Diplock
drifted in and settled down in his armchair with the *Times* crossword. It took him twenty-five minutes to finish it.

"My record is nine minutes thirty seconds," he said. "It's set
by different men on different days of the week. Did you know?
The Tuesday puzzle is always the easiest. The man who sets it
clearly did *Hamlet* and *Midsummer Night's Dream* for School Certifi-
cate."

"I must be one of the few people in England," said Manifold,
"who have never solved a single clue in any crossword puzzle in
my life."

"It's a terrible waste of time," agreed Mr. Diplock. "But then,
most hobbies are a waste of time. Have you got one?"

Manifold abandoned the history test and considered the matter.

"I'm very fond of motor bicycles. I like taking them to pieces
and putting them together again. What about you?"

"I'm a keen photographer. I've got three cameras. A Nikon EL
f/1.4 with a fifty-millimeter lens, a Hasselblad and an Asahi Pentax SV. They all take interchangeable telescopic lenses. I keep
them up in my room. If I brought them down here that oaf G.G.
would probably sit on them."

"Any particular subjects?"

Mr. Diplock said, with a secret smile, "I take a great many pictures of animals in their natural surroundings."

"Like your aunts' goat."

Mr. Diplock looked blank for a moment, and then said, "Oh, yes. I have a number of studies of my aunts' goat. She's a female. But I mustn't disturb you."

When Mr. Diplock had pottered off, Manifold returned to his test, but his mind seemed no longer to be concentrated on it. At a quarter to ten he sighed, got up and put away the papers. They went into the cupboard that had been allotted to him and that still had on the door the neatly typed label "M. H. Mollison, Dip. Ed." The sight seemed to amuse Manifold.

The building now occupied by Trenchard House Preparatory School had been constructed in the form of an E, with a thick backbone, which held all the important rooms, and three thinner wings. Originally it had been a finely proportioned building; but just as the youthful body becomes overlaid in later life with unfunctional and disproportionate excrescences, so had Trenchard House deteriorated in the hands of subsequent owners. A horticultural enthusiast had added a conservatory. A stockbroker had added a billiard room. The final indignities had been committed in 1919, when it first became a preparatory school, and had added to it a number of huts, purchased at knockdown prices from the army. One was now used as a gymnasium by Sergeant Baker; another as a changing room, and a third as a carpenter's shop, under Mr. Bishop, who came up from the village twice a week and watched patiently as boys tortured pieces of wood.

Manifold set out along the corridor that ran right around the building, from the common room at the tip of the southern arm, through the center of the main block and out to the end of the northern arm, which held classrooms on the ground floor and the bedrooms and bathrooms of the resident staff above. He walked slowly, his rubber-soled shoes making no sound on the tiles. From time to time he stopped, as if to get his bearings, or to fix some particular point in his mind. Anyone watching him might have taken him for a burglar, memorizing the layout of a house that he intended to visit later in the dark.

When he reached the northern wing he paused for a long moment, as if debating whether he would go up to his room. Then he opened the side door and stepped out onto the path, crossing it in three quick strides to get onto the grass verge. Then he slid across the lawn and his big figure melted into the summer dusk by the clump of trees that masked the gate into the side road.

McMurtrie, Sacher and Joscelyne shared a turret bedroom at the junction of the north wing and the main block. As seniors they enjoyed various privileges, including that of going to bed half an hour later than the rabble and of turning their light out, within reason, when they liked.

Joscelyne had a copy of a Sunday paper. It was not one which the school would have encouraged, being devoted almost entirely to sexual aberrations. It was sent to him, under plain cover, by one of the housemaids of the aunt with whom he spent most of his lonely holidays. There was a short account in it of the search for Ted Lister. It must have been telephoned to the paper late on Saturday evening.

"They found the kid that night," said Sacher. "It was in the *Express* yesterday. He'd been pretty well mucked about."

"Why do they do it?" said McMurtrie.

"Sadism," said Joscelyne. "Don't you remember they found that cat in the woods behind the village. Someone had strung it up and cut all its legs off. It was still alive when they found it."

"I don't mean that. I mean men going crazy about boys. Look at Connie. Every time he sees Jared he turns bright pink and his knees start to give way."

"It's their bottoms," said Joscelyne.

"They are rather a nice shape," agreed McMurtrie. He was rotating, naked, in front of a small looking glass.

"You're talking nonsense," said Sacher. "It's nothing to do with their bodies. It's psychological. It's based on sex. And sex is based on sadism. And they're both an extension of the power complex. Take T.E.F."

"Take him yourself," said McMurtrie. He was still admiring himself in the glass.

"He's a complete Freudian study. A repressed homo, of course. A lot of schoolmasters are. But in his case I think he really worries about it. You know that old gag about the schoolmaster beating the boy and saying, 'This hurts me more than it hurts you.' With him it might even be true."

"He certainly hurts you," said Joscelyne.

"I think he's impotent," said McMurtrie.

"Whatever makes you think that?" asked Joscelyne.

"If he banged Lucy regularly she wouldn't have to chase everything in trousers that came into this place."

"There might be something in that," said Sacher thoughtfully. "Freud has got a very interesting chapter on the side effects of impotence—"

They heard the squeak of the useful board at the end of the short passage that led to their room. McMurtrie whipped his pajamas out of sight and dived into bed naked. The others followed suit more decorously. Mr. Fairfax opened the door. He said, "When I allowed you to turn your light out for yourselves, I did *not* mean you to hang round talking till all hours. Do you know it's nearly ten o'clock?"

"Sorry, sir," said McMurtrie, pulling the bedclothes up to his chin.

"Well, don't let it happen again. You're meant to set an example to the smaller boys. Good night."

"Good night, sir."

When he had gone, McMurtrie climbed out of bed to put on his pajamas. He was shaking with suppressed laughter.

"What's the joke?" asked Joscelyne.

"Example to the small boys," said McMurtrie when he was able to speak. "I was just thinking. If they had a tape recording of our recent conversation— Hullo!"

He was standing at the window.

"What's up now?"

"It's that new man. Nipping across the lawn like an old stag. I wonder what he's up to."

"I don't fancy *he's* impotent," said Sacher.

5

_____

"To get this down to ninety minutes," said Latrobe, "is going to mean some savage cutting. And the first thing that will have to go will be most of the jokes. The scenes between Sir Toby and Sir Andrew are full of them. I don't doubt the Elizabethan audiences split their sides at mentions of Mistress Mall's picture and Castiliano vulgo, but no one could possibly find them funny now."

"Do you think they were dirty jokes?" said Paxton.

"Probably."

"It'll mean a lot less to learn," said McMurtrie.

"If you analyze the play," said Latrobe, "you'll find that it's a love story mixed up with a Whitehall farce. It's summed up by Viola at the end of Act Two, Scene Two.

'How will this fadge? My master loves her dearly;
And I, poor monster, fond as much on him;
And she, mistaken, seems to dote on me.
What will become of this?' "

"I'm not sure that I've quite worked it out yet," said Sacher. "Who's she meant to be talking about?"

"Her master is the Duke Orsino."

"That's you?"

"That's me."

"And she's in love with you? But you don't know it because you think she's a boy?"

39

"Correct."

"And you're desperately in love with me?"

"That's correct," said Latrobe hastily. "Now I think we'd better read the play right through. I've indicated the cuts by putting pencil brackets round the speeches and scenes I think could be left out."

"I hope you'll be able to give me a hand with the games," said the Commander.

"I'll do my best," said Manifold. "But it's years since I last touched a cricket bat."

"You must have played a few games at your last school, surely. A place up in Cheshire, wasn't it?"

"There always seemed to be a lot of other masters who were much better than I was."

"And what about Kenya? They're pretty hot at the game out there, I'm told. Play it almost all the year round."

Manifold said, a little abruptly, "I'll do what I can. If you loose me on the third game I can't do much harm."

"It'll be a help if you could. T.E.F. lends a hand occasionally, but otherwise it all seems to devolve on Warr and me. Latrobe's quite hopeless. And old Dip prefers pottering round with his camera. Anyway, he's too old."

"How do you all get on together?" Seeing the Commander's look of surprise, Manifold added, "I mean, in a small school like this, all being bachelors and all living in. It would be pretty easy to get on each other's nerves, I should think."

"I wouldn't say that it was an entirely happy ship," said the Commander. "But we rub along all right. After all, we've known each other for some time now. Warr's the newest, and he's been here over two years. Latrobe's been here three. I came five years ago. Old Dip's been here—I don't know—must be at least ten years."

"What about Mollison?"

"Oh, Mollison." The Commander barked out a quarterdeck

laugh. "He was a freak. He came at the beginning of the Easter term. He'd been to one of these teacher training colleges. A complete waste of time, if you ask me."

"Where is he now?"

"I've no idea. Why?"

"Idle curiosity. He isn't in a nursing home, I suppose."

"I don't think it's as bad as that. Resting quietly, I should imagine, and trying to forget One-B. Come to think of it, he was really the fly in the ointment."

"Oh. In what way?"

"Stupid little things. But then, it's always stupid little things that upset people. Give you an example. He had a secondhand car he was very proud of. Spent hours polishing it and tarting it up. You may have noticed that there's only room for four cars in the staff garage. Being the new boy, naturally he was expected to keep his outside. But he couldn't see it. He was always slipping his car in. Then one of ours had to stand out in the open. It became such a sore point—you may not believe this—that when we heard you were coming, the first thing old Dip said was 'Where's he going to put his car?' I can't tell you how relieved we were when you turned up on a motorbike."

"I suppose I'll have to buy a car sooner or later. I shall be pretty broke till I collect my pay at the end of term. What have you all got?"

"Mine's the Cortina. Quite a reliable bus. The Rover is Dip's. It's almost as old as he is. Latrobe's got that Austin 1100, and the open Lotus two-seater, as you might guess, belongs to young Warr."

Manifold said, "When I buy a car it'll have to be old, reliable and easy on petrol."

In the distance Sergeant Baker performed a vigorous solo with the bell.

"Back to the treadmill," said the Commander. "Three-B geography. Thank God it's the last period of the morning. No more classes till Monday."

41

"I get off this one," said Manifold. "I think I'll slip down to the village."

"Oh, Mr. Manifold."

"Yes, Mrs. Fairfax."

"No need for formality. My name's Lucy. And yours, I gather, is Ken."

"That's correct."

"I hope I'm not interrupting you."

Intercepting, more than interrupting, thought Manifold. He had been ambushed on his way to the front door.

"Nothing that matters," he said. "I've got this period off. I was going down to the village to get some cigarettes."

"You can be there and back in fifteen minutes," said Mrs. Fairfax. "Come in and talk. We haven't had an opportunity to get to know each other."

Manifold followed her into the drawing room. Mrs. Fairfax poured out two man-sized glasses of sherry, and sat down on the sofa. Taking the slight wave of her hand as an invitation, Manifold sat down beside her and waited for her to open the bowling.

When it came, it was a fast yorker.

She said, "I'll tell you something, Ken. I don't believe you're a schoolmaster at all."

"You've been listening to One-B," said Manifold. "They think I'm Hitler and Stalin rolled into one."

"I don't mean you don't do the job. I expect you do it very well. I mean that you're not my idea of an assistant master."

"And what is your idea of an assistant master?"

Mrs. Fairfax considered the matter seriously. She said, "Of course, you've got to understand that I'm talking about the sort of schoolmaster I know. I don't mean people who teach in state schools, or even masters at public schools. I mean schools like this one."

"The English preparatory boarding school," said Manifold, "an institution the like of which is not now found in any other country in the world. I doubt if they'll survive here much longer, but they were great fun while they lasted. Sorry. I interrupted you. You were going to give me a thumbnail sketch of the typical prep school master."

"He's educated, but not intellectual."

"No intellectual could tolerate One-B," agreed Manifold.

"He's someone who prefers the company of his own sex, and who's opted out of the world into a snug little retreat, full of men and boys of all ages."

"Like a monk."

"That's right," said Mrs. Fairfax. "Like a monk. Except that one imagines that monks did it for more spiritual reasons. Most men become prep school masters out of laziness. Look at Nigel. The one thing he was good at was games. He was in the Cambridge Rugby football side—fifteen?"

"Fifteen for rugger, eleven for soccer. He didn't get a blue."

"But he was a blue or a half blue at some other game. And he spent so much time playing games that he never got round to taking a degree at all. So what did he do? He drifted into this."

"And will soon be drifting into matrimony, by the look of it."

If Manifold had hoped to provoke some reaction by this, he was disappointed. Mrs. Fairfax said, in the same equable tones she had used throughout, "He's not drifting. He's been hooked. It's pathetic. If that girl offered him a lump of sugar, he'd balance it on his nose and beg for it. If the thing does come off, which it may do if Elizabeth doesn't come across someone who amuses her more, he'll find himself fetching and carrying for the rest of his married life. Have another drink."

She got to her feet, supporting herself with one hand on Manifold's arm as she did so.

"I don't think I dare," said Manifold. "I have to sit next to Cracknell Minor at lunch, and I don't want him starting his Sunday letter to his mother, 'The new master came into lunch absolutely blotto. I could smell his breath.' "

Mrs. Fairfax poured herself out a drink, and stood for a moment with it in one hand, looking down at Manifold. When she had been sitting down, there had been a suggestion of floppiness, the beginning of middle age in a woman who had stopped caring very much about her appearance. Standing, she looked suprisingly vital and by no means unattractive.

"I'll tell you something else, Ken, about the typical prep school master," she said. "He wouldn't have sat on the sofa beside me. He'd have picked the chair which was furthest away and sat on the edge of it, nervously crossing and uncrossing his legs."

Manifold got up, too.

"I wasn't unduly apprehensive," he said. "It didn't seem to me that half-past twelve on a Saturday morning was an appropriate time for a seduction scene. Now I really must be going, or I shall be awarded a double demerit for being late for lunch."

As he closed the door Mrs. Fairfax stood looking after him. An observer would have found it difficult to say whether the expression on her face was one of puzzlement or anger.

"We're supposed to go to church," said Nigel. "Dip gets off by pretending to be an atheist, but the rest of us troop down with the boys. It isn't bad fun. Straight C. of E. and Hymns Ancient and Modern."

"And afterwards?"

"Since you're not master on duty, you'll be free after lunch. Why not come down around teatime and look us up? Elizabeth has told her stepfather about you, and he'd like to meet you. He can't communicate much, but he hears what you say, and can nod his head a bit. Don't come if it would embarrass you."

"It wouldn't embarrass me at all," said Manifold. "I've got a great-aunt who's deaf and dumb. She talks nineteen to the dozen in deaf and dumb language. I've learned to follow it, more or less."

"I don't think Mr. Merriam has got round to that yet. It might be a bit difficult for him. He can only use one hand."

Mr. Merriam's house stood on a corner site by the lane that led up to the church. It was not large, but was a bit more pretentious than the village cottages, and was isolated from them by a stretch of undeveloped building land. Behind the house, in the lane, its nearest neighbor was something that looked like a lumber yard.

Nigel opened the door. He was in shirtsleeves, and seemed very much at home.

"Elizabeth's getting tea," he said. "Come through to the garden and meet the old man."

He led the way through to a room that looked out, through open French windows, onto a smooth stretch of lawn.

"One of my jobs," said Nigel. "Mowing and clipping and weeding. It's the devil to keep it all down at this time of year."

"It's a nice place."

"Until some blighter builds on those plots next door and we have a horde of children squealing on the other side of the hedge. It's all right at the moment. Nice and quiet. Mr. Bishop is our only neighbor."

"Mr. Bishop?"

"Teaches carpentry at the school. He was in the Lion last night. I introduced you to him."

Manifold recalled, out of a medley of characters dimly seen in the public bar on the previous evening, a brown-faced man with a trim beard.

Mr. Merriam sat tucked into a wheelchair under a sycamore at the end of the lawn. At six paces he looked completely normal. It was only when you got closer that you could see the signs that the onset of paralysis had left behind. The left leg dangling, the left hand resting inertly on the arm of the chair; limbs that were attached to but no longer controlled by their owner. The muscles of the face had sagged, too, dragging the cheeks and chin down with them. But there was still a lot of life in the eyes.

Mr. Merriam raised his right arm, which he could control, and shook hands with Manifold, who said, with the emphasis of someone making a momentous announcement, "What beautiful weather we are having. Nice to be able to sit out of doors."

Mr. Merriam signified agreement by nodding his head, and at this moment Elizabeth arrived with the tea things. She cut up two slices of bread and butter into squares, poured out a cup of tea, and put plate and cup on a table close to the right-hand side of Mr. Merriam's chair. Though the attack on his nerves and muscles had crippled the left side of his body, he was still half a man. Using his right hand, he fed himself and drank tea without too much difficulty. Manifold wondered what would happen when the paralysis spread to the other side of the body, but chased the thought away. As with most healthy and insensitive people, the sight of disability embarrassed him but did not touch him.

After a short time even the embarrassment subsided. Elizabeth and Nigel took it in their stride. Their technique, he noticed, was to frame anything they said to Mr. Merriam in the form of a question that could be answered by a nod of the head for yes or a shake for no. On two occasions when Mr. Merriam felt called upon to make an original contribution, he wrote it down on a pad which Elizabeth had put beside him on the table.

The second of these Manifold read, as he passed the pad over. "Has it been mended yet?"

"It's the wireless," said Nigel. "It fell off the table last Sunday and broke some of its parts. Raybould's have promised to let us have it back as soon as possible."

"What he really misses are the news programs," said Elizabeth.

When dusk fell they all moved back into the house and seemed so genuinely anxious for Manifold to stay to supper that he agreed.

"Cold beef, beet root and Lucy's conversation. That's all you'd have got at the school," said Nigel.

"I had some of that yesterday," said Manifold. "A private session."

"That must have been exciting."

"Stimulating was the word that occurred to me." He gave them an edited version.

Elizabeth said, "Do you know, there are times when I feel sorry for her. It can't be much of a life being married to T.E.F. She ought to be living in Chelsea and running a salon."

"With half a dozen lecherous artists competing for her favor," said Nigel.

After supper they took their coffee into the front room and Nigel treated them to a concert, pop and classical alternately, on his record player. Elizabeth prepared a cigar for Mr. Merriam. This was evidently a nightly ritual. She moved a table close to his right hand, made a pile of three volumes of the *Encyclopaedia Britannica* on it, and placed a large table-type lighter on top.

Mr. Merriam did the rest for himself. Using his right hand, he picked up the cigar, impaled the end on a spike at the back of the lighter, put it between his lips, and bending slightly forward, brought the end of it into contact with the flame. It took him a few minutes to get the cigar burning to his satisfaction, but it was clear that he enjoyed doing it for himself. Elizabeth went on talking and seemed not to be watching him, but Manifold noticed that her hand was never more than a few inches from the table during the whole performance.

Manifold was absorbed in contemplation of the puzzles continually presented by human nature. If you took Elizabeth's opinion of Mrs. Fairfax, Mrs. Fairfax's opinion of Nigel, and Nigel's opinion of Lucy, added them together and divided them by the way they actually behaved, it would have puzzled the cleverest mathematician to work out an answer that even began to make sense.

Ten o'clock was Mr. Merriam's bedtime. Nigel pushed the wheelchair up a sloping arrangement of planks on the stairs and then came down again.

"Elizabeth likes to do all the rest herself," he said. "Help me finish up the beer."

"Wouldn't it be easier if he slept on the ground floor?"

"Easier in some ways. More difficult in others. There's no lavatory or bathroom down here. What we'd really like to do is build on a self-contained unit, out at the back. Or if the money won't run to that, we might convert that shed at the end of the garden. It's quite a solid affair. The last owner of this place used it as a workshop, and it's got water laid on."

Manifold said, "It must be a whole-time job for Elizabeth. Running this house, looking after her stepfather, working at the school."

"It's three whole-time jobs. I don't know how she does it. Of course, I do what I can to help. That half-term break was a godsend. Do you know, on that one Saturday I replaced a piece of guttering, unblocked two downpipes, put a new pane of glass in the kitchen window, mended a fuse, put a new flex in the electric iron, clipped the hedges, and mowed the lawn until it was too dark to see. Then I came inside and fixed one of the wheels on that wheelchair."

"Then you went to bed and slept the clock round."

"Don't you believe it. On Sunday— Hullo! Who can be ringing us up at this time of night?"

It was Mr. Fairfax.

He said, "Have you got Manifold with you? Good. I want you both back at the school as quickly as possible."

"What's up?"

"Perhaps you didn't hear the ten o'clock news."

"No."

"Then I'll explain when you get here."

"At eight o'clock this evening, three men believed to be members of a Jordanian terrorist organization broke into the Israeli embassy in Gloucester Gate. They climbed over a wall from an adjoining property and forced a door at the rear of the premises. By-passing the guard in the front part of the building, they made their way up to the offices on the second floor, which were occupied by a cipher clerk and a girl telephonist. The only other person in the building is thought to be the housekeeper who looks after the ambassador's flat, which is on the top floor. They are holding these three people as hostages. The police have cordoned off the building. The ambassador, His Excellency Ben Sacher, was dining with friends. Despite his protests, the police have not allowed him to reenter the building."

Mr. Fairfax said, "I have already had a telephone call from the chief constable. He takes the view that as these people have failed in what was obviously an attempt to kidnap or kill the ambassador, they may very likely turn their attention to his son and use him to bargain for the trapped terrorists. He is sending a police car down here. Since we don't wish to alarm the boys unnecessarily, the police will stay outside and watch the main gate. We shall have to do the rest for ourselves. Until this crisis is over, I would like you to remain, as far as possible, in the school."

"Oughtn't we to be armed?" said Latrobe. He sounded more excited than nervous.

It was Sergeant Baker who answered this question. He said, in tones of unexpected authority, "It's no use fighting these people with their own weapons. What the headmaster meant, I'm sure, is that we must all keep our eyes open. If we spot anything unusual at all, we must pass a message to him, and he can telephone for help."

"That's exactly what I mean," said Mr. Fairfax. "And try to do all this policing inconspicuously. The last thing we want is a panic. Incidentally, I'm arranging to have the morning papers diverted. If anyone wants to know why there are no papers, tell them there's been a strike. That's easy enough to believe nowadays. Now, I'd like to arrange shifts. Commander, could you and Manifold take the first night shift: eleven to two. Mr. Diplock and I will do the middle watch: two till five."

Mr. Diplock groaned.

"And Warr and Latrobe take over until first bell. That means that for once in a way, Warr, you've a chance of being in time for prayers."

Alastair McMurtrie rolled over in his bed and sat up. He wondered what had woken him. Normally he was a sound sleeper.

Then he realized what it was that had penetrated his dreams. It was the loose board at the end of the passage, which gave a sharp and characteristic squeak when trodden on.

Since the short passage outside led only to their room, this meant that someone had approached their door, and since he had heard the squeak only once, it followed that the person must be in the passage now.

Or had he imagined the whole thing?

There was only one way of finding out and at the thought of it he was conscious of a cold feeling in the pit of his stomach and an uncomfortable tightness in his throat. He remembered his father saying, "If you're afraid of something, it's twice as bad if you sit and wait for it. If you go halfway to meet it, it's surprising how it cuts it down to size."

He got out of bed and moved across to the door. Sacher muttered something in his sleep. McMurtrie considered waking him up, but thought: If the whole thing's my imagination, he'll never let me hear the end of it.

He opened the door very softly.

There was a window halfway down the passage, overlooking the front drive. The moonlight, streaming through it, showed him Mr. Manifold seated on a wooden chair, tilted back against the wall, gazing out of the window.

At the click of the door opening, he turned his head and said, "Well, and who is it? McMurtrie? And what do you want?"

"I thought I heard a noise, sir."

"If you heard a noise, it was me."

"Is something wrong?"

"Why should anything be wrong?"

"Well, I mean . . ."

"I am indulging in my hobby of star-gazing. You get a particularly good view of Orion's belt from this vantage point."

A second form materialized at the end of the passage and the voice of the Commander said sharply, "Something up, Ken?"

"It's McMurtrie. He came out to pass the time of day with me, or rather the time of night. Now he's going back to bed, and to sleep. Right, Alastair?"

"All right," said McMurtrie. The thought of Mr. Manifold lurking outside the door had been disturbing. The sight of a second master with him was comforting. He went back to bed and was soon asleep.

6

Colonel Brabazon arrived as the school was finishing its breakfast. He was chief constable of the county; he was also chairman of the governors of Trenchard House School. Mr. Fairfax was glad to see him in both of those capacities.

The colonel said, "I had a teletype on the situation half an hour ago. The gunmen are demanding the release of those two Jordanian girls who tried to hijack the VC10 last March and safe conduct out of the country for themselves and the girls. To say nothing of two hundred thousand pounds, which they describe, if you please, as compensation for false imprisonment. Bloody impertinence."

"Will they get it?"

"Certainly not. They've backed the wrong horse this time. The Israeli government's instructions are absolutely clear. No concessions at all."

"Isn't that going to be unpleasant for their hostages?"

"The Israelis treat all their embassies and consulates as units in their army. The staffs are soldiers on active service. They have to take things as they come. I only wish to God that all governments had the guts to do the same."

"What about the ambassador?"

"He has been told to stay out of it."

"Will he?"

"Ben Sacher's a sound man. He won't disobey his government's orders about not giving way to the terrorists. But he'd like to get back inside and share the danger with his staff. He's tried to get through twice already, but the police wouldn't let him."

"Then all we can do is wait. It makes one feel so helpless."

"Wait and watch. You got my message last night?"

"Yes. We're tackling it in shifts, two of us at a time. We can't keep it up forever, you know. We shall have the masters falling asleep in class."

"It won't last forever. Starve them out or blast them out, it must come to a head inside a day or two."

"And after it's over, what then? There'll be other attacks."

"No lack of madmen in the Middle East," agreed the colonel. "But I shouldn't imagine anything would happen for a bit. These things take time to organize."

"Do you think I ought to suggest to his father that he move the boy?"

The colonel considered the matter. He said, "It's really up to you. He'll be leaving at the end of term, won't he? Five weeks to go. Of course, we could hide him somewhere. Psychologically, I think it would be a mistake. Hiding's always a depressing business. He'll be much happier here with the people he knows."

"If his father agrees, I'll go along with it."

"He's probably as safe here as anywhere. You've got big grounds and the approaches are open. Sergeant Baker's got a walkie-talkie set on the police network. Let him organize the thing. He's a very good chap. I hope he's proving an acquisition to your staff."

For the first time that morning, Mr. Fairfax managed to smile. He said, "He does his job excellently. The only complaint I've heard is that his ideas on physical training are a little old-fashioned."

"He's passing on what he learned at Peel House thirty years ago."

"In fact, I wouldn't mind keeping him on permanently."

"He's getting close to his retiring age. Might be managed. I'll have a word with his superintendent." The colonel made a note. "Your other man's proving a distinct acquisition, too."

The colonel, who was already at the door, stopped. "What other man? Oh, you mean Manifold. He's nothing to do with us. As far as I know, he's a perfectly genuine schoolmaster. Actually, I don't know a lot about him. He was recommended to me by a friend. When I heard you needed someone quickly I got the friend to contact him. I'm glad he's turning out well."

A final thought occurred to the colonel. He said, "I suppose you'll have to tell young Sacher what's happening. But it would be a good thing if you could keep it from the other boys. We don't want a panic."

"I've taken steps already," said Mr. Fairfax. "The papers have been stopped and the school television set is temporarily out of action."

"Pretty thrilling, isn't it, sir?" said McMurtrie.

"Isn't what thrilling?" said Manifold cautiously.

"What's happening at the embassy. I mean, not very nice for Jared, but exciting for everyone else."

"Do I understand that everyone knows everything about it?"

"Of course they do," said Joscelyne. "There are at least three undercover transistors in the dormitories. It was all on the news. Anyway, we knew there was something up before then."

"First it was you and G.G. camping out in the passage," said McMurtrie. "And I must say you gave me no end of a fright. You might have warned us what you were up to. Then Shepherd, going to the lav at six o'clock this morning, turned a corner and ran slap into Connie, prowling round the corridors carrying a sort of knobkerrie. I don't know which of them was more frightened."

"Then we saw the chief constable's car coming up here after breakfast—"

"And the head sent for Jared. He's still there—"

"And the television in the library seemed to have disappeared."

"And something seemed to have happened to the papers we usually get in the morning—"

"And so," said McMurtrie, "we slipped straight down to the kitchen and borrowed her copy of the *Sun* off Annie. There's a sensational photograph on the front page. I can easily get hold of it again if you'd like to look at it."

Monty Gedge, who was both stout and silent, spoke for the first time.

"I saw a film once," he said. "It was about a school on the Northwest frontier. It was threatened by tribesmen. They armed all the boys with guns."

"What happened?" said Manifold.

"A lot of people got shot."

"The same thing would happen here," said Manifold.

"So I gather you know all about it already," said Mr. Fairfax.

"Yes, sir," said Sacher.

"I had underestimated the power of the pocket transistor. In the circumstances, I think we had better restore the television set to the library and all listen to the news as it comes in."

"Yes, sir."

"Would you—I mean, are you quite happy to go on as usual?"

The only previous occasions on which Mr. Fairfax could remember isolating a boy was when he was suspected of having an infectious disease or was about to be expelled.

"I don't think it would improve the situation," said Sacher, with a smile that seemed almost entirely adult, "if I had to spend the next few days in the sick room."

"I don't suppose it would. I needn't say how sorry I am. I suppose you knew some of these people."

"Mrs. Penberthy, the housekeeper, has been with my father for as long as I can remember."

There was a story behind that, Mr. Fairfax knew. Ben Sacher's wife was not dead. She had left him shortly after Jared was born. She was now living in Cairo.

"And I knew both the cipher clerks. Torbah and Haresh. I

55

don't know which of them was on duty. Torbah only came to us this year. He's nineteen. I hope it isn't him."

Mr. Fairfax said nothing.

Sacher said, very politely, "Do you think I had better go back now? Mr. Manifold must be wondering where I am."

"The situation at the Israeli embassy was largely unchanged at midday today. The ambassador, His Excellency Ben Sacher, was allowed by the gunmen to speak on the telephone to the chief cipher clerk, who is one of the hostages. He reported that they had none of them been harmed, and had so far been well treated. The police cordon round the building has been maintained and traffic passing either side of the building has been diverted.

"The ambassador has repeated his offer to go into the building and negotiate with the gunmen, but it is understood that his government has categorically refused to allow this. It is in any event doubtful whether the British authorities would agree to such a move.

"If there are any further developments, we shall be interrupting the sports program at three o'clock this afternoon with a bulletin—"

"A rotten show," said Commander Gaze. "But what can you expect with a government of weak-kneed old women?"

"What would *you* do?" said Mr. Diplock.

"I can tell you what I wouldn't do," said the Commander. "I wouldn't truckle to terrorists."

"But what would you *do?*"

"When I was in Malta, in 1931, a crowd of stokers mutinied. Barricaded themselves in the seamen's club and refused to come out. Reggie Lyon was Senior Naval Officer Malta at the time. He had the guns of the *Renown* trained on the club and gave the bastards half an hour to make their minds up. They knew Reggie. They were out inside ten minutes."

"I don't think," said Mr. Diplock, "that we could get a battleship close enough to the Israeli embassy to be effective."

"I must emphasize," said Mr. Fairfax, "that I'm not going to have the school demoralized or the routine upset. If there is to be a further bulletin, I will allow One-A to go into the library, in an orderly fashion, at five minutes to three in charge of the master who is taking them for second period. As soon as it is over they will return to their classroom with him and get on with their work. There will be cricket, as usual, for all three games, at four o'clock. I would suggest that discussion of the matter be discouraged, particularly among the smaller boys."

The hindquarters of a handsome bay mare faded from the screen and was replaced by the face of the newscaster. Before he opened his mouth it was clear that the news was not going to be good.

"We interrupt our program of racing at Lingfield," he said, "to give you up-to-date news of the siege at the Israeli embassy in Gloucester Gate. As was mentioned in our previous bulletin, communications had been established by telephone with the terrorists. It is understood that their spokesman has given the police an ultimatum. Unless their terms have been agreed to by eight o'clock this evening, the three hostages will be shot. It is believed that the terrorists, who belong to the fanatical El Arish organization, will take their own lives if this is the only alternative to capture. They have offered to release the hostages in exchange for the ambassador, whom they now admit to have been their main target. The ambassador, His Excellency Ben Sacher, has been in constant touch with his government and our own foreign secretary. Both governments are standing by their earlier decision that he cannot be allowed to hand himself over to men who have avowed their intention of killing him. We shall be letting you have further news as soon as it becomes available."

His anxious face faded and an excited voice said, "They're coming into the straight now. Red Socks has his nose in front of Paramatta. Can he keep it up? It's going to be a very close thing. . . ."

In silence seven boys and Latrobe watched Red Socks hold on to win by a nose in the three o'clock race at Lingfield. In silence they trooped back toward the One-A classroom.

Latrobe put a hand on Sacher's arm to detain him and motioned the rest of the boys to go ahead. He said, "I just wanted to tell you how much I admire you. You're being tremendously brave about all this."

"What's there to be brave about? I'm not going to be shot."

"If there's anything I can do to help."

"I think the others will be waiting for us."

Sacher removed his arm unhurriedly from Latrobe's grasp and walked off down the passage.

"I wish someone would break a window or something," said Mr. Fairfax. "Teatime was horrible. Hardly anyone talking. Everyone munching steadily with one eye on Sacher and the other on the clock."

"I can't see any reason to get worked up about it," said Lucy coldly. "The only person really concerned is that boy and he seems to be the only one who isn't behaving hysterically. Yes, Elizabeth, what is it?"

"Patterson's been sick. He's the third."

"Then mop it up."

"I have."

"Then what are you bothering me about?"

"It was really Mr. Fairfax I wanted. I think someone ought to say something to them."

"Why? Small boys are always being sick. It's probably something they ate at tea."

"I don't think so. It was when Holbrow said, 'Have they shot them yet?' that Patterson turned round and was sick all over the floor."

"I'll come and talk to them," said Mr. Fairfax. "This has got to stop."

"I'd wallop the lot of them," said Lucy. "That'd stop them worrying about other people's troubles."

Mr. Fairfax was not actually running, but he was coming along so fast that the three boys in the turret room knew that he had something important to tell them.

"It's all right," he said, as soon as he got into the room.

The three boys sat up in bed.

"At least, it's more or less all right. Much better than might have been expected. It was all on the nine o'clock news. We'd have got you down to listen but we didn't want to miss any of it. Apparently your father knew that there was a way in over the roof of the next house. It was a sort of fire escape from the embassy. He persuaded the police to go in that way with him. They got all the hostages out that way. They were locked up in the kitchen in the top-story flat. Then they went down and tackled the terrorists. There was some shooting. One of the policemen was wounded. And one of the terrorists was killed, and both the others were wounded."

"That's good, isn't it?" said Joscelyne.

"Lovely," said McMurtrie. He could picture guns roaring, bullets flying, bodies falling. As good as television. Like television, too, the baddies got killed and the goodies only got wounded.

Sacher was sitting bolt upright in bed, his face very white. Mr. Fairfax looked at him curiously, said good night, and went out and shut the door.

Sacher turned over on his face and started to cry. The other two boys watched him, with sympathy, but without embarrassment.

7

—————————

"What I'm giving you," said Chief Superintendent Anderson, "is a preliminary report. We've been at it for ten days now. The results haven't been sensational. But they haven't been altogether negative, either."

He had an audience of four. Colonel Brabazon, chief constable of Hampshire, was at the head of the table. The other three men were Fred Lowry, deputy chief constable of Surrey, Chief Superintendent Woolmer, representing the chief constable of Sussex, and Chief Superintendent Brayne, representing the chief constable of Kent.

"We started off with a bit of good luck and a bit of bad luck. The good luck was that a witness actually saw the car leaving the scene of the crime. The bad luck was that he wasn't a mite more observant."

They had had another piece of bad luck, too. Out of respect for Fred Lowry, Anderson didn't mention it. The case of Sergeant Callaghan was still sub judice.

"From what that witness told us, we do at least know what we're *not* looking for. It isn't a very large or new or expensive car. And it isn't a sports car. It's an oldish family-type four-door saloon."

"That narrows it down to five million," said Brayne.

"We know rather more about it than that. In fact, when I go through the scientific evidence, I think you'll agree that if we find the car we shall be able to identify it without any doubt at all."

"Find the car, find the man," said Lowry. The others grunted agreement. That was the common sense of the matter.

"Before I deal with that," said Anderson, "I'd like to clear up one point. The scientific evidence has established, beyond any reasonable doubt, that the same man was responsible for the killing of Jackie Fenton in Rewell Wood last September and Barry Lathom in Winterfold Forest in April of this year. The similarities in the three cases had already raised a supposition that it was the same man, although there was always the chance that it was imitation killing. What we now know is that in every case, including the present one, the man took a blanket out of the car and spread it on the ground. There were fibers on the boys' clothing in each case. Coarse gray woolen fibers. I've got the laboratory reports here if you want to look at them. They've done a lot of work on those fibers. They established, quite early on, that the blanket was army surplus. The sort of thing that was sold off, after the war, by the hundred thousand. At that point one had to accept the further possibility that different men had the same sort of blanket. Not likely, but possible. Now they've given us something else. In all three cases they've isolated microscopic fragments of—"

Anderson peered at the paper in front of him.

"Distemonanthus benthemiamus."

"Come again," said Lowry.

"It's a sort of wood. All I can really tell you about it at the moment is that it's a hard wood, and is No. 64 on the Chatterton Key Card."

"Might be used by carpenters or cabinetmakers," suggested Colonel Brabazon thoughtfully.

"It might indeed, sir."

"I think that conclusively links the three crimes. You'd agree with that?"

The others nodded.

"Then from this point the investigation can be considered,

officially, as covering all three. There'll be a number of administrative matters to settle on that. But we needn't waste time discussing them now. Carry on, Superintendent."

"I'd like you to take a look at the map here." Sheet 182 of the inch-to-a-mile Ordnance Survey had been pasted to a piece of hardboard, with sections of the surrounding sheets attached to it. It covered a square from a point east of Aldershot to Tonbridge in Kent, then south to Eastbourne and along the coast to Bosham, south of Chichester.

On the map were three red circles. The first was north of Cranleigh and included Winterfold Heath, Winterfold Forest and Hunt Wood. The second, away to the south, enclosed the area bounded by Warburton, Madehurst and Arundel. The third circle was a larger one. It covered Haydock Wood, where Lister had lived, Tolhurst Green, where he had been picked up, and Brading, where he had been killed. The A-24, running south from Horsham, cut this area into two almost equal halves.

Anderson said, "This man's followed the same technique in all three cases. He takes his car out around dusk. Not when it's actually dark, but when it's beginning to get dark. He must, superficially, be a sympathetic or harmless-looking character, because boys are pretty leery nowadays of accepting lifts from strangers. Anyway, he gets a boy into the car, terrorizes him, probably by showing a knife or a razor, ties him up, and dumps him in the back of the car on the floor. I'll tell you how we know that in a moment. Then he drives him somewhere quiet and gets to work on him.

"In the first two cases he took care to pick a lonely spot. Rewell Wood, north of the Arundel–Chichester road, is overgrown and full of gullies and pits. It was two months before Fenton's body turned up. Winterfold Forest is a lot more open. We beat through it and found Lathom inside the week. This last time our man seems to have worried even less. He just dragged Lister into the first field that was handy."

"And next time," said Lowry, "he'll take him to the bottom of his own garden and leave him lying about on the lawn."

The others nodded agreement. They were all acquainted with the curious mentality of series killers who took diminishing precautions, which could be calculated almost in arithmetical progression. Was there not inscribed in every policeman's pocket book: "The second murder is three times as easy"?

"There'll be no next time," said Anderson. He said it with such absolute conviction that the four men looked at him.

"In the first two cases we got very little out of the scene of the crime. As I said, it took us two months to locate Fenton and exceptionally rainy weather had washed away most of the marks. In Lathom's case, there were signs that a car had been driven to the spot. Snapped off undergrowth and a bit of oil. The ground was rutted and muddy and we might have got some useful prints. Unfortunately we had that hard frost the day before."

"Third of April," said Brayne. "Killed off all my young dahlias."

"This time it's quite different. The ground was reasonably soft and we were there soon enough to prevent it being disturbed. We used about a ton of plaster on that piece of ground, and I reckon there wasn't a blackbird landed there in the twenty-four hours before the murder that we don't know all about. If you'd care to look at this plan, you'll be able to follow it better. The car drove up to the gate and stopped. The man got out and opened the gate—marks there, and there—got in again, drove through, turned the nose of the car to the left and then backed for ten yards down the track as far as the corner there. We think he left the gate open, in case he had to make a quick getaway. Then he got out, opened the back door and dragged the boy out, by his shoulders. There was a tiny shred of dark-blue leather in the metal eye hole of one of his gym shoes and another thing we found, on the shoes and the clothes, were dark-gray fibers with fragments of rubber, or rubberoid. They must have come from the mat in the back part of the car. But most useful of all, when the boy was dragged out of the car, his body must have made contact with the edge of the coachwork and we got some paint."

"Give the lab boys a flake of paint," said Brayne, "and you'll keep them happy for a week."

"We didn't send it to the laboratory. We sent it straight up to Home Office Central Research Establishment at Aldermaston. They've put it under the mass spectrometer and this is their report. Three separate layers of paint. Dark green, light-gray undercoat, dark-gray finish. And a rusty discoloration *under* the light gray."

"That seems clear enough," said Colonel Brabazon. "A car which was originally dark green, got a bit shabby and rusty, and was resprayed. First with a light-gray undercoat, then with a dark-gray finish."

"It takes us even further than that," said Anderson. "The boffins broke down the dark-green paint into its original constituents, and compared it with the check samples they keep on file there. The car was one of the standard BMC range, probably an Austin or an MG, and certainly pre-1967."

"Because they stopped using that sort of paint?"

"No. Because they stopped using that sort of floor carpet."

"It's still a pretty wide field," said Lowry.

"I've been keeping the best to the last. We got perfect impressions of all four tires. They're cross-ply, which is common enough, but"—he paused for effect—"the nearside rear tire has got a plug in it."

"A plug," said Brayne. "That's illegal."

"There are garages who will still do it. They say they're doing it for the spare tire. Don't use it unless you have to. But there are still quite a few plugged tires in use. However, taken in combination—"

"You've made your point," said Colonel Brabazon. "If we find the car, we'll be able to tie it to the crime tight enough. Where are we going to look for it?"

"We can make a few broad assumptions as a starting point. First, I don't think a man like this drives hundreds of miles. That would mean a very long absence from his home base and would increase the risk of questions being asked. But he goes a fair way. Far enough to get away from people who might recognize him or his car. The second point is that when he does pick up the boy, he's much more likely to drive away from his base than towards it."

"Sound psychology," said Colonel Brabazon.

"If you take the three points where the bodies were found, join them to the points where the boys were picked up, and extend them inwards for forty or fifty miles"—he demonstrated on the map—"that brings you into an area roughly here. You can't do an exact resection, of course. It's only an indication. If any one of our assumptions is wrong, we could be a hundred miles out either way."

The four men considered the proposition in silence. Among them they represented more than a hundred years of criminal investigation; of reading the minds of men and women who, from a bewildering variety of motives—mania, passion, vanity, greed or whim—had started to defy the laws of the land.

Lowry said, "I think it stands up, but I'd be happier if we had one witness who identified the car positively."

Anderson said, "Yes." They were on delicate ground again. With a prompt warning he could have had his own network in operation and they might have known a lot more about the car. They might even have intercepted it on its way home. "Apart from old Mr. Moritz," he said, "we've got four witnesses. I'd put three of them in the probable-but-not-proven category. The fourth one's different. They all noticed a dark-gray oldish saloon car at about the place we think it should have been, but their versions of who was driving it are—well, you shall hear for yourselves."

He opened a folder and extracted four documents. "Mrs. Grover, who lives at Tolhurst green, and is married to one of the cricketers who was playing there that afternoon, noticed a car of this type when she was coming towards the cricket ground from her house at about six o'clock. She had the impression it had stopped near the ground to pick someone up. She couldn't swear it was a boy in it, but she thought she caught a glimpse of someone sitting beside the driver. She had the impression that the driver was a woman."

His audience all looked up. Anderson continued smoothly.

"A Mr. Parsons, who had been drinking at the Three Horseshoes at Brading—that was the pub, you will remember, that young Maybury and his girlfriend were using—came out at about a quarter past ten and had to wait to cross the street because a dark saloon car was coming towards him. Now, that timing is very interesting. Old Mr. Moritz left the pub at ten o'clock. It was later than usual, and he and the landlord both remembered it."

"*And* Des Maybury," said Brayne. "It's in his statement. The boy must have had one eye on the clock by that time."

"Why?" said Colonel Brabazon.

Brayne said, with a chuckle, "He wanted the old man out of the way, sir, so that he could get on with certain plans he had for Rosie."

"Of course. Then we can accept ten o'clock as a confirmed time. Please go on."

"The point is this. We know it took the old man half an hour to make it back to the cottage. The point where Lister's body was found is roughly halfway there. That puts him there at ten-fifteen, when he saw the car coming out. Now, it wouldn't take a car more than a minute to reach the village, and cars aren't common on that stretch of road at night."

"Right," said Lowry. "Ten to one it was the same car. Did Mr. Parsons spot the driver?"

"He did," said Anderson. "He said it was a man. Beyond the fact that he thought he was wearing glasses, he couldn't give any real description. But he was quite clear about that. They were steel-rimmed glasses. He caught a reflection of light flashing from them."

"Anything on the car?"

"Nothing that we hadn't got already. He only had a quick, sideways view of it. The next one is Mr. Mason. He, too, was coming home from his local at about half-past ten—or maybe a bit before. He had to step aside for a car at that crossroads—there. After passing him, the car turned to the right. If we've read our man's mind correctly, he turned *away* from home when he came out onto the road and saw he was spotted, but he'd want to get back onto course as quickly as possible and this crossroads is exactly where he would turn. He'd make his way south towards the B-272, take any of these minor roads—here—and come out near Cowfold."

"The timing's a bit slow," said Brayne. "That crossroads isn't more than three miles from Brading. He wouldn't take fifteen minutes to cover three miles. Not if he was in a hurry."

"Agreed," said Anderson. "But remember that Mr. Mason wasn't too definite about the time. He said it was *about* half-past ten. Probably a little earlier."

"And he wouldn't go blinding along a secondary road," said Lowry. "The last thing he'd risk was being involved in an accident. I'd mark that one as short of certain, but highly probable."

"The fourth," said Anderson slowly, "is very interesting indeed and it does check out the other three. You see that building, just off the B-272, marked as Southerns Farm. The farmer's wife was expecting a baby, getting close to zero hour, and she was on a regular round which the district nurse, a Miss Colman, was making. Miss Colman struck me as a very sensible and observant witness. And she was particularly good on times, because she had to keep a log of her visits. She came out of that track from Southerns Farm at about ten-forty. As she got to the entrance a saloon car, which was passing her, going west, had to pull into the left to avoid one of those monster lorries, which was coming the other way."

"And no doubt sailing along on the crown of the road," said Colonel Brabazon bitterly.

"I think it must have been. Because Miss Colman said that the saloon car had almost to stop and to get right into the verge. She was one of our first informants, bless her. She saw one of our notices, telephoned us at once, and we were down there by midday on Sunday. We got some tracks from the gravel along the verge. They're not very clear, but if you look at these photographs . . ."

"That's the brute," said the colonel. "Not a shadow of doubt. You can see his paw marks. That's the cross-ply tire and that's the plug in the nearside wheel."

"And the driver?" said Lowry.

"Definitely a man. He was wearing light wash-leather gloves. She saw his hands on the steering wheel. She, too, noticed that he was wearing steel-rimmed glasses. And she says that his hair was whitish and fluffed out. Almost as if he was wearing some sort of wig. She got much the best view of him, because she was sideways on to him, and her own headlights were directed towards the car."

"Good enough to recognize him again?"

"I'm afraid not. She was quite firm about that. All she got was a quick impression. Hands, glasses, hair."

"A pity," said the colonel.

"There's another thing," said Brayne. "Isn't it possible that he'd disguise himself a bit? You remember that chap in the Isle of Wight who went after boys. He used to dress up in the most fantastic way."

"It certainly sounds as if he might be wearing a wig," said Lowry. "And you can get plain glass spectacles from any theatrical costumier."

"I'm afraid it's very likely he was disguised," said the colonel. "Now let's see what we have got. A man, age uncertain, shoe size . . ."

"Between nine and ten. And judging from the depth of the impressions, between ten and twelve stone in weight, although it's dangerous to try to be too accurate about that."

"Might wear glasses. Might have white hair. Or might not.

Could be a carpenter or cabinetmaker. It's not much to go on, is it?"

"We've picked up some fibers from a tweed jacket which could be matched up."

"They can be matched up *when* we find him," said the colonel grimly. "Now, what's your plan?"

"I think the car is our best chance, sir. And the way to find it is to comb the likely area. I don't think it can be east of Billingshurst or west of Chichester. And I'd take a line through Petworth as the southern boundary and through Cranleigh as the northern one."

As he spoke he was penciling in the lines on the map.

"It's a big area, I agree. And full of private houses. And there are other possibilities, too. Garages, car dumps or simply a lonely shed or barn. I'll need all the men you can let me have. If we don't strike oil soon, we'll have to consider broadcasting a description. But it's a two-edged weapon. It might bring in the information we want, or it might frighten the man so much that he takes the car, strips it and dumps it in some gully where we won't find it for years."

At this point, Chief Superintendent Woolmer cleared his throat. Everyone looked at him. The colonel said, "You've been very quiet, Les."

Woolmer said, "I've been quiet because I've been thinking."

The other three grinned. Leslie Woolmer was a personality. He played chess at international level and had tied for fifth place that year in the Hastings congress. He was also a scientist of more than average ability. He was one of the men who had perfected the technique of using laser beams to produce holograms, or three-dimensional pictures. A month before, he had used his holograms to demonstrate to a jury that a husband must have walked across the carpet in a bedroom he swore he had never entered, and strangled his wife as she lay in bed.

"Let's have it," said the colonel.

"It was this idea of the man dressing up. Were you thinking

that if he wore a white wig and a pair of glasses it might make him look a kindly sympathetic old bugger? The sort that a boy wouldn't be afraid to take a lift with?"

"I was thinking of it mainly as a disguise. Something to hide his identity. But I suppose it might work that way, too."

"If he was a bit of an actor, and used to dressing up, mightn't he have gone further than that?"

"Meaning what, Les?"

"I mean," said Woolmer, "that he might have had *two* disguises. He might have started out dressed up as a woman. A boy would have even less hesitation in accepting a lift."

There was a moment's silence. Then Anderson said, softly, "It's an idea. And it would mean that we could accept the first identification along with the others. I've always been puzzled about that one. Mrs. Grover struck me as a good witness, and the timing was exactly right."

"It's like a lot of other ideas we've been discussing," said the colonel. "We can prove them all quickly enough when we locate our man. And I agree that the best way to find the man is to find the car. Let us have details as soon as possible of the men you can put onto the job. We'll split the area into station sections and coordinate the search with the local men. They're the ones who'll know the form. I'll have the chairman of the Chichester bench standing by, in case anyone proves obstructive and we want a search warrant quickly. And I'd like a word with you, Andy."

When the other three had gone, the colonel said, "I couldn't help noticing that you didn't say anything in front of the others about that bit of paper you picked up. You know what I mean."

"I know what you mean," said Anderson.

"Why not?"

"I thought long and hard about it. It's not that I doubt their discretion. I needn't tell you that. But I had two reasons for keeping that one piece of evidence between ourselves for the moment. The first was that there's nothing the others can do to help us with it. We're doing all we can about it already."

"I agree with that," said the colonel. He smiled as though at a private joke that they shared.

"My second reason was this. Once they heard about it, their reaction—maybe a quite unconscious reaction—would be to ease up on this general search. I don't want that. I want it to be slow and thorough and to cause as much commotion as possible. I want our man to hear it coming. To feel it closing in on him. I want him to lie awake at nights, thinking about it. I want him to be frightened. I want him to sweat."

"What you mean," said the colonel, looking curiously at Anderson's face, "is that you want him to feel a little of what he dealt out to those three boys."

The Scotsman gradually relaxed. The colonel could see the fire dying down. Anderson said, "It's daft to suppose that you don't have personal feelings when you're on a job like this one."

8

"I think the colonel's right," said Sergeant Baker. "Those people took a bad knock at the embassy and it'll take them time to reorganize."

"We certainly can't keep the staff up all night and every night," said Mr. Fairfax. "It wouldn't be fair on them or on the boys."

"The way I look at it is this," said the sergeant. "I don't think they'd want to kill young Sacher. That couldn't do them or their so-called cause any good. The object would be to kidnap him. Bring pressure to bear on his father, and through his father on his government."

"Yes," said Mr. Fairfax. He hoped that he sounded as matter-of-fact about it as Sergeant Baker. He had just missed the war, leaving Wellington a month before V-E Day. He sometimes thought that if he had had some experience of the war it might have made certain things easier to take. He became aware that he had missed something the sergeant was saying.

"I'm sorry," he said. "Could you say that again."

"I was saying, if they want to kidnap him, they'll need a car. And there's only two ways you can get a car inside these grounds. One's by the main gate at the head of the drive. The other's by the side gate, on the Rudgwick Green road. What I think we ought to do is ask the police to have a standing patrol at the main gate, and put a chain and padlock on the side gate."

"Suppose they leave the car some way away and come in on foot?"

"Can't guard against everything," said the sergeant. "My guess is they'd try to bring the car as close up as possible. If we're wrong, we're wrong, and that's all there is to it."

What an extraordinarily robust and self-reliant man Baker was, thought Mr. Fairfax. In some ways he reminded him of his own father.

"How many times have I told you," said Mr. Bishop. "Measure twice, before you cut once. And if in doubt, measure too big, not too small. You can always take half an inch off a piece of wood. You can't add it on."

"Sorry," said Monty Gedge. "I suppose it means I'll have to start again."

"It means you've ruined a nice piece of wood, Gedge. And nice pieces of wood are getting scarcer all the time. I read the other day that a square mile of forest is cut down for every edition of a Sunday paper that comes out. Carry on like that, and soon there won't be any wood left. Then what'll happen?"

"Everything will be made of plastic," said McMurtrie. He was constructing an elaborate affair of wood and metal which looked like a rabbit hutch equipped with all modern conveniences.

"That's right," said Mr. Bishop. "Plastic. First we had the stone age, then the iron age. We'll finish up with the plastic age."

"Plastic's useful for some things," said Joscelyne. "Toothbrush handles, for instance."

"Thermos flasks."

"Lavatory seats."

"Plastic lavatory seats aren't nearly as comfortable as wooden ones," said Gedge.

"When my father was in Canada," said McMurtrie, "he stayed at a hotel in Winnipeg and they had hollow lavatory seats and used to run warm water through them, just imagine."

"That's enough about lavatory seats," said Mr. Bishop. "Kindly bear in mind that your parents are paying five pounds a term extra for you to learn carpentry."

The carpentry class was a popular one, and most of One-A had got into it. It not only made a nice relaxed break in the routine, but had the advantage of producing something to show for it by the end of term. Pipe racks, bookcases, knife boxes and picture frames, all useful solutions to the birthday and Christmas present problem.

Mr. Bishop moved softly from job to job, giving out much sound advice and occasional help. "If you don't seal up those joints a bit neater," he said, "your astronauts are going to be in for trouble in the stratosphere, aren't they?" This was to the Warlock twins, who were constructing a spacecraft. "Run some plastic wood in, wait till it's good and dry, and sandpaper it off."

He moved round to McMurtrie and stood watching him as he bent over what he was doing, his handsome, half-formed face flushed with the effort. Then Bishop said, "If you hold a chisel like that you'll never make a smooth job of it." He put one hand gently on the back of McMurtrie's, gave the chisel a half turn, picked up the mallet with his other hand and awarded the handle of the chisel a smart tap. It slid smoothly forward.

"It's easy enough when *you* do it," said McMurtrie.

"Everything's easy if you do it the right way," said Mr. Bishop.

"That's a set of photographs I took last sports day," said Mr. Diplock. "I got them with my Pentax using a fifty-five-millimeter lens and a shutter speed of a five hundredth."

"I think they're very good indeed," said Manifold.

It was the quiet hour after lunch, and they were alone in the common room. The photographs were, in fact, excellent. Mr. Diplock was not only using a very good camera, but he knew how to use it, and had the additional advantage of knowing his subjects. The close-up, taken with a telescopic lens, of Marsham Minor's face as he just managed to scrape over the high-jump bar, was a masterpiece of the action photographer's art.

"You must have been doing this for a long time," said Manifold.

"When I decided to take up schoolmastering," said Mr. Diplock, "I decided that the greatest danger to be avoided was boredom. Once you have conducted two or three successive generations of boys from cover to cover through Kennedy's Latin primer and Hall and Knight's algebra, the job has no more variety than that of the man who fastens the same nuts onto the same bolts on a conveyor belt."

"A little more variety, surely. Not all boys are the same."

"Boys are either intelligent or stupid. And can be further subdivided into those that are hard-working and those that are lazy. In combination, that gives you four possible types, and no more. I have diverted from what I was saying. In order to avoid boredom, you need a hobby. And the hobby must be geared to your means. I started by collecting butterflies. That demanded only a butterfly net and a killing bottle."

As he said this Mr. Diplock's eyes showed a momentary gleam of excitement, and Manifold saw a younger and more active Mr. Diplock creeping through the bushes, a net in one hand, his steel-rimmed glasses flashing.

"That lasted for some years. I then turned to postage stamps and amassed a very large and completely worthless collection. It filled several suitcases. After that came coins. And now I have reached what I think might justly be described as the apotheosis of all hobbies. Photography. There is one simple prerequisite. If you wish to take good photographs you must be prepared to spend a lot of money on a good camera. You need a number of gadgets, of course, and a grasp of certain techniques. But these are less important than imagination—and luck. My best photographs have always been the result of grasping the lucky moment. This one, for instance . . ."

"Good heavens," said Manifold.

It was a photograph of Lucy Fairfax. It was in close-up, and it was clear from the set of her lips that she was saying something unpleasant. There was something else about the picture. It had a surface gloss behind which the face seemed to be imprisoned, like a goldfish in a bowl.

"How on earth did you manage to get it?"

"I happened to notice that when she stood in a certain position by the door leading into the garden, her reflection was thrown very clearly onto the dining room window. In the ordinary way it is almost impossible to take a satisfactory picture of a reflection in plain glass. If there is any light in the room behind the window you get no picture. And if there is too much light in front, the light itself reflects off the glass. An interesting technical problem. It took me a month to get that picture right. Here is another. I took that with a telescopic attachment in the early morning."

It was Commander Gaze, halfway round the field on his early morning run. His lips were drawn back from his teeth, and a very small trickle of saliva was running from the corner of his mouth.

"You wouldn't have imagined that he was enjoying himself, would you?" said Mr. Diplock dryly. "The most interesting photographs are always those that show animals in their natural state, don't you think?"

A thought occurred to Manifold. He said, "You haven't got one of me, I suppose?"

"I took it two minutes ago," said Mr. Diplock. "When you were studying that last photograph. I used a remote-control device. The camera is on the shelf over there."

Manifold said, "Good God!" and was saved from further comment by the bell for afternoon school.

" 'Come hither, boy,' " said Latrobe. " 'If ever thou shalt love, In the sweet pangs of it remember me; For such as I am all true lovers are, Unstaid and skittish in all motions else, Save in the constant image of the creature That is beloved. How dost thou like this tune?' We'll have someone playing on some sort of musical instrument while I'm saying that. You're meant to be listening to it, but most of your attention is on me."

"O.K.," said Joscelyne.

" 'How dost thou like this tune?' "

" 'It gives a very echo to the seat Where love is—love is' something or other."

"Throned."

"Sorry. 'Where love is throned.' "

" 'Thou dost speak masterly. My life upon't, young though thou art, thine eye hath stayed upon some favor that it loves. Hath it not, boy?' "

" 'A little, by your favor.' "

" 'What kind of woman is't?' "

" 'Of your complexion.' "

" 'She is not worth thee, then. What years i' faith?' "

" 'About your years, my lord.' "

" 'Too old, by heaven! Let still the woman take An elder than herself. So wears she to him. So sways she level in her husband's heart. For, boy, however we do praise ourselves, Our fancies are more giddy and unfirm, More longing, wavering, sooner lost and won, Than women's are.' "

" 'I think it well, my lord.' "

" 'Then let thy love be younger than thyself, Or thy affection cannot hold the bent. For women are as roses, whose fair flower, Being once displayed, doth fall that very hour.' "

" 'And so they are; alas, that they are so! To die even when they to perfection grow!' "

"You'll have to see if you can put just a bit more feeling into it. Remember that I'm making love to Olivia, by proxy, but *you're* making love to *me.*"

"They must have felt awful nits," said McMurtrie.

"Oh, why?"

"Spouting all that stuff to a boy dressed up as a girl. I mean to say, if you make love on the stage nowadays, you do at least get a girl to do it with, if you see what I mean."

"I see what you mean," said Latrobe, "but I don't agree. When you're acting, you don't think of the other people on the stage as themselves. You think of them as the characters they're playing."

"And anyway," said Joscelyne, "when you see them close up, they're absolutely smothered in makeup. I sometimes wonder how people kiss on the stage without sticking together."

"I once saw a love scene being shot in a film," said Billy Warlock. "The girl was yellow. Absolutely bright yellow."

"Drink it up," said Elizabeth.

"It's such muck," said Paine.

"Your parents have paid for this tonic. You're going to drink it and like it."

"Last time, it made me feel sick."

"Nonsense."

"It isn't nonsense. I jolly nearly was sick."

"Are you going to do what I tell you, or not?"

"I don't see why I should."

"I'm not going to stand here all day holding this spoon. If you don't drink it, I shall—"

It suddenly occurred to Elizabeth that she had no idea what she would do. Most of the boys did what she told them, but she had no actual authority. Paine was a lout. She had had trouble with him before, but never outright defiance. Paine recognized the strength of his position, too. He smirked and said, "If my parents have paid for the tonic, it belongs to me, doesn't it? And I can do what I like with it, can't I?"

"You can drink it and stop arguing."

"Mrs. Fairfax told Holbrow that all you were here for was to give her a hand. I don't see why you should boss us about. Annie doesn't boss us about."

Elizabeth flushed scarlet and took a step forward. Paine saw that he had gone too far. He decided on tactical retreat. "Oh, all right," he said. "I'll drink the beastly stuff, even if it does make me sick."

"And why should you, if it upsets you?" said Mrs. Fairfax, from the door. It was not clear how much she had heard.

Elizabeth said, "Since you're here, you can give it to him yourself."

She placed bottle and spoon carefully down on the dispensary table and marched out.

"Paine said *what?*"

"As far as I could make out, he was quoting Lucy as saying that since I ranked with the kitchen maids, there was no reason why he should do what I told him to."

"I see," said Nigel. "I see. Well, I've had my eye on that young man. This time he's definitely gone too far."

"Don't make a fuss with Lucy. She'll only deny she ever said it, and I shall look a perfect fool."

"I've no intention of saying anything to Lucy," said Nigel.

He marched upstairs to the bedroom that Paine shared with three other boys. They were sitting up in bed listening to some story Paine was telling them, which they seemed to be finding amusing. When they saw the look on Nigel's face the chattering ceased abruptly.

"I understand that you've been impertinent to Miss Shaw," he said.

Paine said, "I didn't mean anything, sir. Really I didn't."

"It's perfectly clear what you meant. You behaved like an ill-bred guttersnipe, and I'm not going to have it. Do you understand?"

"Yes, sir."

"Get out of bed."

"Yes, sir."

"And bend over."

Nigel picked up a slipper.

Paine seemed about to make some protest, but the look on Nigel's face silenced him. He folded himself obediently over the end of the iron bedstead.

9

"So Paine sneaked, did he?" said Nigel.

"He was still crying when I went up last night to say good night. I insisted on him telling me what had happened. You must have hurt him a good deal."

"I meant to hurt him," said Nigel. He was still angry. "I don't suppose, by any chance, he told you what he had done."

"He said something about some medicine which he hadn't wanted to take. It didn't seem to me to be anything very serious."

"It was nothing to do with the medicine. It was what he said. He told Elizabeth, to her face, that she was only one of the maids, that there was no more reason for him to do what she told him than if she was Annie or cook."

"He said that?"

"He certainly did. And he quoted your wife as his authority for saying it. I don't imagine you're going to support him, are you?"

"I'm certainly not supporting him. It was a rude and stupid thing to say. Quite apart from being untrue."

"You realize that Elizabeth can't continue to work here unless she has your backing. Your full backing."

"I do realize that," said Mr. Fairfax. "I have always given it to her and I always will give it. But that is not the real point. I made it absolutely clear, when you came here, that no boy was to be beaten, except by me."

"You made it perfectly clear, Headmaster. And for more than

80

two years I've observed your ruling. This was an exceptional case, and it won't happen again."

"I'm glad to have your assurance on that point."

"All the same, I think it's a bad rule."

"Indeed? Why?"

"I don't mean that masters should go round as they used to, I believe, in the old days, with a stick in one hand and a Latin grammar in the other."

"I'm glad you don't think that," said Mr. Fairfax, who was also getting angry.

"But I think if the boys knew that if they went too far they'd get it hot and strong, on the spot, they'd behave themselves a lot better. And save everyone a good deal of trouble."

"Perhaps you'll forgive me for pointing out," said Mr. Fairfax, "that saving masters trouble is *not* the primary object of education."

"It may not be the primary object," said Nigel, "but if they were allowed to get on with the teaching without having to spend half their time putting down riots, a lot more knowledge would get imparted in a much shorter time."

"I'm not prepared to argue about it."

"You may not want to argue, but you ought to think about it. And while we're on the point, I suppose you realize that if he'd been given a bit more authority, Mollison would be happily teaching here, not sitting at home nursing a nervous breakdown. You ought to consider your responsibility to your staff as well as to the boys."

"I think that's an entirely unjustifiable criticism."

"Then perhaps you'd explain why."

"I've no intention of explaining anything. I've laid down a rule, and if you don't agree with it you have a very simple remedy."

"I thought it would boil down to that," said Nigel. "Do what you're told or get the sack. It still seems to me to be a rotten argument."

"Excuse me if I'm interrupting a momentous discussion," said

Mrs. Fairfax, making one of her catlike entrances.

"What is it?"

"Mr. Tennyson has arrived. I have put him in the dining room."

"Mr. Tennyson?"

"No relation to the poet, he assures me. He telephoned on Monday. He has two boys he would like to entrust to us. He is taking up a post in the Persian Gulf."

"Oh, yes. I'll come right along. I think we've said enough about —what we were discussing."

"I think so, too," said Nigel.

"You know," said Mrs. Fairfax to Nigel, "Miss Shaw has really no need of a knight in armor to fight her battles for her. She is perfectly capable of looking after herself. More than capable, believe me."

Nigel stalked out without a word.

"You appreciate," said Mr. Fairfax, "that it was originally built as a gentleman's private residence. We've kept it that way as far as possible."

"It's a fine house," said Mr. Tennyson. He was a thin, fit-looking man, so tall that he had to stoop to get through the doorways of the little rooms on the upper floor.

"It means, among other things, that we have no conventional dormitories. This is one of the largest bedrooms, and it only takes five beds. It's for the little boys."

"Things have certainly changed since my time," said Mr. Tennyson. "If I'd brought back a teddy bear and taken it to bed with me, I don't think I should ever have lived it down."

"Boys are more babyish in some ways," agreed Mr. Fairfax. "More grown up in others."

"The older boys have rooms to themselves, I imagine."

"Not actually to themselves. Watch your head as you come up here. We're in what must, I think, have been the servants' quarters."

"That's another thing that has changed, isn't it? Having servants, I mean. Who sleeps along here?"

"Three of the senior boys."

"It's very snug."

Mr. Tennyson looked approvingly round the turret room, with its scrubbed wooden floor and its three white iron beds, each with a red and white striped blanket. There were no teddy bears here. Joscelyne had the makers' plan of a Ferrari Dino pinned up over his bed. McMurtrie had a picture showing equally interesting construction details of a young lady wearing a minimum of clothes, who had been photographed, for reasons known only to herself and her personal publicity agent, lying on top of what looked like an ironing board. Sacher had a pile of books on the shelf above his bed, and beside the books a photograph.

"I know that face," said Mr. Tennyson. "Surely it's Ben Sacher."

"It is. I expect you saw in the papers about that business at the embassy."

"I did indeed," said Mr. Tennyson. "It was lucky it came out the way it did."

"It certainly was. Now, if we go down these back stairs they will bring us out in the north wing and I can show you some of the classrooms."

"I hope you're not going to get the sack on my account," said Elizabeth.

"I don't think so," said Nigel. "I wouldn't say that T.E.F. and I parted the best of friends, but on the strict understanding that I never do it again, I think I've been forgiven this time."

"I wish I could have seen you do it," said Elizabeth. "Nasty little beast. I should have enjoyed watching it." She kissed him very warmly.

"He was remarkably well behaved in geography class this morning. Who was that chap T.E.F. brought round?"

"A prospective parent, I believe. Why?"

"I thought I recognized his face, that's all. Maybe I saw it somewhere in the papers."

"I think you were absolutely right," said the Commander. "When I joined the navy snotties were regularly beaten by the senior sublieutenant, and it never did them any harm. Do you know, I believe it's that same tin of terrible biscuits."

"Let's take them out and bury them," said Warr. "Then we might get some decent ones."

"You're talking nonsense," said Latrobe.

"If there are none left, Lucy will *have* to open a new tin."

"I'm not talking about biscuits. I'm talking about beating boys. How can you sit there, smugly saying that it never did them any harm? How do you *know* it didn't?"

"Because they all turned out to be damned good chaps in the end," said the Commander.

"And how can you tell that?"

"Because I happened to fight alongside them in the war. Of course, you'd be too young to remember much about that."

"You're evading the issue. Tell me how assaulting a boy who's too small or too frightened to resist can do either of you any good."

"Aha. I thought we should get onto the old trick-cyclist line soon. You're going to tell me that corporal punishment is all bound up with sadism and sex and does the perpetrator more harm than the victim."

"Since you press me," said Latrobe, "that's exactly what I was going to say."

"And so," said the Commander, who wasn't really listening to him, "if a parent lays a hand on his children they run screaming to the NSPCC. If a schoolmaster beats a boy he sues him for assault. And the end result of all this flabbiness and evasion of responsibility is a generation without moral standards or physical guts."

"I have never in all my life," said Latrobe hotly, "listened to such fascist claptrap. You're elevating physical violence to a moral virtue."

"Well, I must say that I agree with G.G.," said Warr. "Look at the way students are behaving. What do you think, Ken?"

"I think it's like fox-hunting," said Manifold. "All the practical arguments are in favor of it and all the moral arguments are against it."

"What do you think, Dip?"

"It's no use asking me what I think," said Mr. Diplock, "unless you define what you're talking about. So far you've raised four quite distinct questions and answered none of them. Do I think that corporal punishment raises moral issues? Certainly not. It is an arbitrary method of maintaining law and order and has no more moral basis than confining a soldier to barracks for not cleaning his buttons. Do I use it myself? No, I don't. I have more sophisticated ways of maintaining control. Do I approve of the way students behave? Certainly not. I think they are cutting off their noses to spite their scholastic faces. Was there one other point? Oh, yes, these biscuits. There I entirely agree. They should be taken out privily, after dark, and buried. I would suggest the asparagus bed. They would make an excellent mulch."

After tea that day, finding himself off duty, Manifold decided to stroll down to the village. He did not go by the direct route, down the drive and onto the main road, but crossed the corner of the lawn and came out under the shadow of the cedar of Lebanon which the nabob had planted with his own hands two centuries before, and which had now spread until it overshadowed path and lawn with its umbrella of boughs.

Here he paused for a moment. From a distance he might have been thought to be admiring the tree, but a close observer would have seen that he was looking beyond it, at the thick row of shrubs that masked the high iron fence and at a wilderness of bushes which had once been a formal sunken garden, now abandoned as being beyond the efforts of the one gardener and boy employed by the school.

The side gate was now equipped with a stout chain and a heavy padlock, but the gate was unchained at the moment. He opened it and stepped out onto the side road. Ahead of him lay the tangled miles of Tinmans Common. A right turn would have brought him back to the main road. Instead, he turned to the left. He was now skirting the gardens that lay behind the school and formed an important item in its prospectus. ("The School grows all of its own vegetables and much of its fresh fruit in its own kitchen gardens and orchards.")

At the end of the garden, Manifold turned to his left, using the footpath that ran along the outside of the wall. This brought him out into a lane which he recognized as the one leading to Mr. Bishop's wood yard. Beyond it he could just see the roof of Mr. Merriam's house, at the point where the lane ran out into the main road.

It seemed he was going to turn into the lane, but changing his mind at the last moment, he crossed it and kept along the path. This brought him out at the west end of the church. Here he turned left, passing between a row of new-looking council houses and a Georgian rectory which was keeping to itself behind a thick yew hedge, and emerging eventually into the main street of Boxwood village, slumbering peacefully under the late afternoon sun.

His objective was Mr. Raybould's wireless and general electrical shop, a small, dark, cluttered establishment, presided over by Mrs. Raybould.

"Mr. Merriam's wireless set?" she said. "I'm afraid we had to send it up to Reading. In a terrible mess it was. The old gentleman must have fairly sent it flying off the table. I expect he was trying to get at it, to turn it on. He'd be likely to be awkward, poor soul."

"How long do you think it will take to get it mended?"

"You never can tell nowadays, can you? If they have to send

back to the makers for parts, it might take quite a time. It does seem a pity, seeing as how it's one of the few things left he can enjoy."

"Would it be possible to hire one for him?"

"Hire one?"

"One of your sets." Seeing the look of doubt in her eye, he added, "My name's Manifold. I work up at the school."

"Ah, I thought I recognized you. I saw you walk past with young Mr. Warr. The one who's courting Mr. Merriam's step-daughter."

So much for Nigel's idea of keeping his intentions secret, thought Manifold. One of the disadvantages of living in a village was that everyone knew everything about everybody.

"I'd be happy to put down a deposit," he said. "If this one got broken I'd pay the difference."

"Well, if you'd be willing to do that," said Mrs. Raybould, "it certainly would be a kindness for the poor gentleman."

They chose a sturdy-looking battery-operated set and Manifold carried it back down the main road to Mr. Merriam's house.

When he rang the doorbell, nothing happened. This was odd. It seemed unlikely that Mr. Merriam would be out. And he remembered that Elizabeth had told him that when she was not there, the woman from the house next door kept an eye on things. He rang the bell again.

At this point Mr. Bishop appeared at the side gate. He said, "It's no use ringing. Mrs. Loveday just slipped down to the shops. When she does that she always asks me to keep an eye open. Being next door, it's no trouble."

Manifold reflected that there was something to be said for living in a village after all.

"The key's under the mat. Why don't you let yourself in? That's a new set you've got there. Mr. Merriam *will* enjoy that. He used to have that old set going all day. You'll be just in time for the six o'clock news."

Mr. Merriam seemed pleased to see him. He wrote on his pad,

"Beer in the corner cupboard." They listened to the news in companionable silence. It seemed to be mostly about cricket. Manifold was finishing the beer when Elizabeth arrived, admired the wireless set and opened a fresh bottle. While they were washing the glasses she said, "Really, you put us to shame. Of course we ought to have done it ourselves. But near the end of term we're all pretty broke."

"I happened to have a bit of money," said Manifold. "That's because I sold my car before I came here. By the way, I hope you haven't been having any more trouble."

"Trouble?"

"With Lucy."

"Oh, her." Elizabeth paused, glass in one hand, dishcloth in the other, to consider Mrs. Fairfax. She said, "Sometimes I loathe her. At other times I feel deeply sorry for her."

"I'm not sure which sentiment she'd find more provoking," said Manifold.

Elizabeth looked at him curiously. "You're an odd fish," she said. "You don't really belong in this outfit at all, do you?"

Manifold said, "You're the second person who's told me that."

"Who was the first?"

"Lucy. She had me in for a tête-à-tête. No, she didn't make a pass at me. She said I wasn't in the least her idea of a prep school master. Her main reason, I gathered, was because I sat on the sofa beside her instead of perching on the edge of the chair furthest from her."

Elizabeth laughed so much that she nearly dropped the glass she was washing. It was a reasonably funny remark, but Manifold had the impression that she was awarding it more laughter than it deserved.

That same night, at a few minutes before midnight, Commander Gaze came padding home across Tinmans Common. He was following a path that he seemed to know well, switching direction without hesitation when it forked, and coming out almost immediately opposite the side gate of Trenchard House.

The fact that it was padlocked did not seem to disconcert him.

He moved down the road about fifty yards until he found the gap in the iron railing that he was looking for, squeezed through it, skirted the tangle of the old sunken garden, and made his way straight across the lawn, heading for the side door in the west wing.

Much of the space between the bulge of the northwest turret and the side door was taken up by a lean-to under which the staff parked their cars. As he approached it, his feet making no noise on the grass, he thought he saw a flash of light inside the lean-to.

It was the sort of light that might have been shown by someone using a pencil flashlight with great discretion.

As he watched, it came again. No doubt about it. There was someone there.

The Commander paused to take stock of the possibilities. Another member of the staff putting away his car. Impossible. He would long ago have heard the car coming in by the main gate and down the drive. A boy fooling about. Possible, but unlikely. A burglar seeking to steal one of the cars. Equally possible, but equally unlikely. If he did succeed in getting it started, how was he going to get it out of the grounds? The side gate was padlocked, the main gate under observation by the police.

Well, there was one way of finding out.

The Commander stepped onto the gravel of the path, crunched across it and said in his most authoritative voice, "Who's there and what are you up to?"

This produced no reaction of any sort.

The light, he thought, had come from between the two cars in the center, his own Cortina and Latrobe's Austin. He took a step forward, and as he did so a dark form rose on his left and crashed straight into him. Whoever it was, he was heavier than the Commander and a more skillful infighter. A fist hit him in the face and a knee drove hard into his stomach. Then his ankles were hooked from under him and he fell backward, hitting his head on the side of the Cortina.

Thinking about it afterward, he was unable to decide whether he had lain there for ten seconds or ten minutes. His next clear recollection was of finding himself on his hands and knees on the gravel path.

Blood from a cut on his forehead was trickling down his face. Still feeling dizzy, he crawled across the path and sat down on the edge of the lawn, his head between his knees.

After a minute he felt steady enough to get his handkerchief out of his pocket and wipe away the blood. The bruise on the back of his head was beginning to throb painfully. It seemed to be the only serious damage.

He hauled himself to his feet and moved toward the side door. What to do next? He could, of course, wake up Mrs. Fairfax and demand medical attention, but he shied away from the thought of the explanations that would follow. Best to see if he couldn't patch himself up. The dizziness was passing and he felt better already.

When he reached his own room he saw that there was a light shining under Manifold's bedroom door. He knocked and went in.

Manifold, in pajamas, dressing gown and slippers, was perched on the edge of his bed smoking a cigarette. He said, "Hullo, G.G. Come in." And then, "Hullo, hullo! What have you been up to?"

The Commander started to tell him. When he got as far as the light in the shed, Manifold jumped up, said, "Wait here," and disappeared from the room.

He was back in five minutes. He said, "The cars all seem all right. No sign of whoever it was. No point in running after him. Be a mile away by now. Let's see if we can do something for that cut. Better wash your face first."

He got a roll of adhesive tape and some scissors out of a drawer, examined the cut critically, said, "I'll dab a bit of this disinfectant on. No stitches needed, I fancy." He soon had the Commander patched up. Then he got out a bottle of white tablets and said, "I should take a couple of these. You'll sleep like a baby, and feel much better in the morning."

"You seem remarkably well equipped to deal with accidents of this sort," said the Commander.

"Had to look after ourselves in Kenya," said Manifold. "You push off to bed."

When the Commander had gone, Manifold washed his own hands carefully, took off his dressing gown, kicked off his slippers and climbed into bed. But it was some time before he went to sleep.

10

The three boys were sitting on the edge of Joscelyne's bed, which was the one nearest to the window. Outside a moon was lighting up the grounds of Trenchard House, a moon so full and golden that it seemed to be giving out heat as well as light.

"It's like being on one of those platforms," said Joscelyne, "right up in the roof of the theater, where they work the spotlights. Roger and Billy took me once."

"There's that owl again," said McMurtrie. A white shadow had drifted across and disappeared into the top of the cedar.

"It almost makes you believe in God, doesn't it?" said Sacher. *"Almost.* Don't you always?"

"Sometimes," said Sacher. "Sometimes. Do you think he'll come tonight?"

"It's four days now. We'll give it another ten minutes."

Ten minutes had gone, and another five, and McMurtrie was on the point of saying, "Well, I'm going back to bed," when Joscelyne grabbed his arm. A figure was crossing the lawn.

"It's G.G.," said Joscelyne. "No mistaking him."

"Pacing the quarterdeck," said McMurtrie.

"Hornblower in person," said Sacher.

"What *can* he be up to?" said McMurtrie. "He can't be on the booze. All the pubs will be shut by this time."

"Hold it," said Joscelyne. "Here comes the next one."

A second figure had emerged from the shadows and was now crossing the lawn.

"Our Mr. Manifold," said McMurtrie. "Following G.G. Just like he was last time. What can *he* be up to?"

Sacher said, "I meant to tell you, but somehow I forgot. It was when all that business was on up at the embassy. You know T.E.F. sent for me. He had Colonel Brabazon with him, so I had to hang about outside. I heard a good deal of what they said."

"Well?"

"Did you know Sergeant Baker's really a policeman? He's here to keep an eye on me."

"Stale."

"We'd guessed that years ago."

"Go on."

"Well, T.E.F. said something about Mr. Manifold having been put in as an extra precaution to help Sergeant Baker for the rest of this term."

"I thought as much," said McMurtrie complacently. "Didn't I tell you, Jos?"

"If you thought that, you were wrong. He's not. When T.E.F. said that, the colonel sounded quite surprised. He said, 'Oh, he's nothing to do with us.' "

"Then what the hell is he doing here?" said McMurtrie.

Joscelyne said, "I suppose he could be what he says he is."

"Nonsense," said Sacher. "He's no more a schoolmaster than my Aunt Hepzibah. We could easily find out. Let's go and search his room."

The three boys looked at each other. It was a night made for excitement and discovery.

"We'll be beaten for sure if we're caught," said Joscelyne.

"Why should we be caught?" said McMurtrie. "It's only on the floor below. Manifold and G.G. are safely out of the way. Connie's the only other one who sleeps in that passage. If he comes out and catches us, all Jared's got to do is give him a sweet smile and he'll buckle at the knees and won't say a word."

Sacher punched him absent-mindedly in the stomach while they considered the project.

"We'll never get another chance like this," said McMurtrie. "Count me in."

"I suppose I could always plead I was led astray by evil companions," said Joscelyne.

"Bring your torch," said Sacher. "We might as well do the job properly."

The three boys crept along the passage, stepped carefully over the creaking board at the end, and went down the narrow back stair that led to the floor below. Here, too, the moonlight was flooding in through the windows, filling the place with light.

The room at the end of the passage was Latrobe's. They stood outside his door for a moment and were relieved to hear a gentle rhythmic snore.

"Beautiful, isn't it?" whispered McMurtrie. "Like a purling brook."

"Tonsils, most probably," said Sacher. "Come on."

They opened the door of Manifold's room and peeped in. The windows here were on the other side and the moon was masked. The flashlight came into play.

"Don't shine it out of the window, you goat," said Sacher. "Keep it down on the floor."

"It's spooky, isn't it?" said Joscelyne. "Now I know just how burglars feel."

"I expect they get used to it," said Sacher. "Just like any other job, really." He was much the coolest of the three. "If there's anything here at all, it'll be in one of those small drawers in the chest, I should imagine. What we're looking for is papers. They might give us a clue."

The right-hand small drawer contained nothing but handkerchiefs and socks. The left-hand drawer turned out to be locked.

"Well, that's that," said Joscelyne. "Let's get back to bed."

"I'm not sure," said Sacher.

"What are you trying to do?" said McMurtrie. "If you bust it open it'll be obvious—"

"I'm not going to bust anything," said Sacher. "It's a rickety old piece of furniture and I believe . . ."

As he was speaking he removed the right-hand drawer completely and laid it on the bed. Then he put his hand in, got his fingers underneath the end of the left-hand drawer, tilted it and pushed.

It came open.

"Hey presto."

"Nothing in it but an old pullover," said Joscelyne. "What a swindle."

"There's something wrapped up in the pullover," said McMurtrie.

It was an automatic pistol, with a bulbous black attachment on the end of the barrel. The three boys stared at it in fascinated silence.

Joscelyne said, in a whisper, "Wrap it up again and put it back, quick."

There was no argument. Three minutes later they were back in their own room.

"What are we going to do?" said McMurtrie.

"We ought to tell someone."

"Who?"

"And what?" said Joscelyne.

It was a difficult question. They debated it for some time.

"The fact that he's got a gun doesn't actually *prove* anything," said Sacher. "Lots of people have got guns nowadays."

"It's against the law."

"Not if you've got a license."

"Why should a schoolmaster have a license? They only give them to policemen and people like that."

"If we do tell T.E.F., we'd have to tell him how we found out," said Joscelyne. "Then we'd be for it, no question."

They thought about this.

McMurtrie suddenly gave vent to an enormous yawn. He said, "We'll talk it over in the morning. We'll think of something to do."

In a very few minutes they were all three asleep; too fast asleep to hear the Commander, who returned an hour later, or Mani-fold, who was later still. Only the owl in the cedar tree saw them.

"Arrangements for our annual cricket match against St. Catherine's tomorrow," said the headmaster to the school, assembled after breakfast. "Boys who have already notified me will be allowed out with their parents from twelve o'clock. The game will start at two-thirty. You are encouraged to bring your parents to watch it, but it's not obligatory. However, tea in the marquee will be for boys *with* parents only. In other words, the possession of a parent constitutes a tea ticket. Any boy in One-A or One-B not actually playing or with a parent can come in and help to hand round. And I *mean* hand round, Gedge."

This was a reference to the occasion a year before when Monty Gedge had attached himself to a plate of cucumber sandwiches and eaten the lot.

"Anything else, Mr. Warr?"

"Nothing, Headmaster. Except that this year I suggest we might win the match for a change."

"Agreed. Yes, McMurtrie?"

"What about the carpentry class, sir?"

This normally took place at twelve o'clock on Wednesdays and Saturdays.

"We'll have to postpone that. We'll see if Mr. Bishop can work in an extra hour next Monday. You might go down in break and tell him."

"Right, sir," said McMurtrie. And later, to Joscelyne and Sacher, "I thought it would work."

"What are you going to do?"

"What I said. I'll want all the twopenny pieces we can raise."

A quick check produced three.

"It should be enough," said McMurtrie. "I'll go the back way, and that'll give me plenty of time."

The back way involved crawling through the overgrown shrubberies of the far side of the school grounds, squeezing through a very narrow gap in the iron railings behind them, crossing the first side road, jumping the ditch and pushing through the hedge on the far side of it, following a path between allotment gardens and finally emerging almost opposite Mr. Bishop's house and wood yard.

McMurtrie, on an occasion when he had been left behind at school for the first week of the holidays, had worked out this route as a quick and unobtrusive way of getting into the village.

He found Mr. Bishop at the back of his yard. Having given him the message about the change in times, he stopped for a few moments to look round. It was a place he was very fond of. There were stacks of cut and uncut timber, an array of circular saws, automatic planers and sizers and heaps and heaps of fresh sawdust all over the floor. The smell was entrancing. Lucky Mr. Bishop, to work in this heavenly place and not in some depressing factory.

"You're after sweets, or would it be cigarettes?" said Mr. Bishop.

In the past he had acted as purveyor of both for the boys in his class. It was an additional reason for taking up carpentry.

"Neither this time, your right reverence," said McMurtrie. "I've got some telephoning to do."

"A girlfriend, I expect."

"Naturally."

The telephone kiosk was a few yards up the side road. It was immediately opposite the big shed that stood at the bottom of old Mr. Merriam's garden. No danger of poor old Mr. Merriam seeing him. He would be anchored to his chair in the back room. Elizabeth might have spotted him if she had been there, but he was pretty certain that she was up at the school. Even if she saw him, he doubted if she would report him. He didn't rank her with the Establishment.

The telephone kiosk was empty. McMurtrie arranged the three twopenny pieces carefully on the ledge beside the telephone, lifted the receiver and dialed a number.

It was a number that he had been told to remember and not to write down. When the pips came he pushed in a coin and a woman's voice said, "Hullo."

To his relief he recognized it. It was his father's secretary, a competent but kindly middle-aged Scotswoman called Miss Lindsay. She said, "And what can we do for you, Master Alastair?"

"Do you think I could have a word with my father? And if you have to fetch him, please fetch him quickly, because I've only got two more twopences."

"It would take more than four pennyworth of time to reach him just now. When we last had word of him he was in Beirut."

"Oh, dear."

"He's due back any day. Is there something I can do for you?"

McMurtrie thought quickly. Miss Lindsay was discreet and reliable. He said, "What I wanted someone to do was to check up on one of the masters at this school."

"I see."

Miss Lindsay sounded unsurprised.

"He says he was at a school called Broughton House."

"Spell it."

"I'm not sure, but I think it starts B-r-o-u-g-h."

"A preparatory school?"

"Yes. It's in Cheshire. And it closed down at the end of last term because of drains."

"That shouldn't be too difficult. Has he a name?"

"Hold on while I put in another twopence. Yes. His name's Manifold. Kenneth Manifold."

"And if I get any information, would you like me to telephone you?"

"You can't do that. Mrs. Fairfax—she's the headmaster's wife —she listens in to anything anyone says on the school telephone. Could you write it to me?"

"I'll do that."

"Thanks awfully."

When McMurtrie had rung off, Miss Lindsay sat for a few

minutes thinking. There were only two agencies of any standing that dealt with preparatory schools, and she felt sure that an inquiry to one or the other of them, backed by the authority of her office, would quickly produce the information that young Alastair required.

But she was not only discreet. She was also knowledgeable. She knew a good deal of what went on in the block of offices overlooking St. James's Park underground station. After a few moments of reflection, she rejected the outside telephone and dialed instead a number on the internal line.

The voice that answered was young and cheerful. She said, "Would you mind coming up and having a word, Tony? Something rather odd has just happened."

11

"Raymond would have loved to be here, but he's in Kuwait."

"Herbert will be with you next term. His weak point is his hips."

Taken separately, these observations would have needed handling. Running neck and neck, they taxed even an experienced headmaster's wife like Lucy. She managed to bestow an understanding smile on Mrs. Shepherd, indicating concern for Herbert Shepherd's hips, and said to Mrs. Paxton, "Goodness, he must be hot."

"The temperature in summer reaches a hundred and four in the shade. And the humidity approaches a hundred percent."

"Poor man! Poor you, too! Having to cope with everything at home."

Seeing she had lost her audience, Mrs. Shepherd switched to Elizabeth, who was trying to fill up the bowling analysis page for a keen but inexpert scorer, and said, "He dislocated them when he was two, and they never really set properly."

"Why have I got too many dots?"

"You don't count wides and no-balls. They go somewhere else. I'm sorry, Mrs. Shepherd. You were telling me about Herbert."

"It *is* difficult," said Mrs. Paxton. "It's a big house, and it takes a good deal of running. With both boys away at school, and Raymond abroad so much, well, it positively rattles. I've got a girl who comes in by day to do the rough work, but . . ."

"But you're all alone at night?"

"Except for Tommy."

"Tommy?"

"Our Alsatian."

"Oh, I see. He must be a great comfort. I seem to remember Terence telling me that you were rather isolated."

"A hundred yards from the main road. And with all these unpleasant men about . . ."

"I wouldn't care for it," said Lucy. "Every time you open the papers you seem to see about some wretched girl or child who's been assaulted."

"Yes, indeed," said Mrs. Paxton, who had been steering the conversation in this direction with the skill to be expected of a barrister's wife, so that she could produce her tidbit at the appropriate moment. "We had the *police* round only two days ago about that."

"About what?"

"Do you remember that horrible case, near Horsham, about a fortnight ago? The boy who was tortured and then killed?"

"Of course. Yes," said Lucy absently. "I thought they'd caught the man."

"Not yet. But they know a lot about him. Confidentially"—Mrs. Paxton leaned toward Lucy and away from Mrs. Shepherd—"they know roughly where he lives and they know *all* about his car. The make and the color, and things like that. And they're searching every conceivable place until they find it. They looked in our garage, and an old shed at the bottom of the garden, and beat through the woods. I believe they've got more than *two hundred* men on the search."

"Four," said Elizabeth. "Tick it off in the box and put it down in the analysis. That's right. You're getting the hang of it, aren't you?"

"I think I can do it myself now, Miss Shaw."

"Take it away and try. There's another four."

"They seem to be making a lot of runs," said Mrs. Shepherd.

"They've about twice our numbers," said Elizabeth. "And the boys always seem to be so big. They're a Roman Catholic school, of course."

It was a theory, firmly believed at Trenchard House, that Roman Catholic schools, in some crafty papistical way, succeeded in holding on to their pupils to a greater age than Protestant establishments, and that this accounted for the fact that they always seemed to win their matches. There was a story, current in the lower forms, that on one occasion the St. Catherine's fast bowler had actually sported a mustache. Whatever the truth of the matter, their run of success had been unbroken for the last five years.

When Nigel had suggested that they might reverse the trend, he had not been speaking solely out of hope. There were reasons for his optimism. He himself was an excellent cricketer and a sound, if rather impatient, coach. And for once he had good material to work on.

McMurtrie and Paxton were passable bowlers, good enough to keep the opposition scoring down to a reasonable total. Sacher was a flashy bat and a remarkably agile slip fielder. But the stars of the team were the Warlock twins. Their father, Peter Warlock, was not only an actor. He was a cricketer of ability who captained the Stage Cricket Club and had featured in numerous charity matches. Roger and Billy were following in his footsteps, not because of any hereditary flair, but because their father had determined to make them into cricketers. He had had them coached in the Christmas holidays at an indoor school, and in the Easter holidays at the nets at Lords.

In the corresponding match in the previous year, which had been played at St. Catherine's, they had failed to come off. Roger had been clean bowled in the first over by the one unplayable ball of the match and Billy, who followed his twin in most things, had been out five runs later. Now, with another twelve months of experience behind them, thought Nigel, who was umpiring at one end, they might see something rather different. At this point the larger and more aggressive of the St. Catherine's openers edged a ball to Sacher, who caught it competently. As the batsmen walked toward the pavilion, Nigel caught sight of a car turning in at the gate at the bottom of the ground. He wondered who it could be. Cars were normally parked in the yard behind the school. They were discouraged from coming onto the field.

He saw Mr. Fairfax lever himself out of his deck chair and walk to meet the intruder. The car, which was a big Daimler, circled slowly and came to rest alongside the pavilion. Evidently a privileged parent. Mr. Fairfax was shaking him warmly by the hand.

As the fielders crossed over, Sacher said, "Just like my father to drive slap onto the ground."

"Is that really your father?" said Nigel.

"That's right, sir," said Sacher. "And I bet those two chaps with him are goons."

"A little more to your right for middle and leg," said Nigel. "Six balls to come. Play."

The new batsman hit a soft catch back to McMurtrie, and departed for the pavilion, looking sheepish.

"We seem to be doing a bit better this year," said Mr. Fairfax to Ben Sacher. "That was a very nice catch Jared held. Do you know Colonel Brabazon, our chairman?"

"We haven't met," said Sacher. "I'm glad to have the opportunity." He was a small man, but undeniably impressive. The brown hair had streaks of gray in it and there were deep lines running down on either side of his mouth to the corners of his chin, but these were the only signs of worry or strain in a face of remarkable serenity and power.

"Good of you to find time to pay us a visit," said Mr. Fairfax. He glanced for a moment at the young man who was standing a yard behind Sacher and wondered if he was going to be included in the introduction. Apparently not. The other young man had got back into the car and was sitting in the passenger seat, with the window rolled down.

"It's a pleasure to get out of London," said Sacher, "and a double pleasure to come to a place like this, in weather like this."

He looked round the wide field of smooth-shaved grass, framed by lines of two-hundred-year-old elm and beech; at the white-clad marionettes performing in the middle; at the groups of little boys in bright blazers lounging on rugs and watching the game; at a solitary horse poking his head over the dry-stone wall from the next field, watching the boys. A lazy, enjoyable ritual, which meant nothing and proved nothing. What was at the back of it? A refusal to look facts in the face, or a refusal to be frightened by them? Complacency or common sense? Compared with his own arid, vital country, where boys were laborers at fourteen and soldiers at sixteen, this was an absurdity. Had he been wrong in letting Jared have any part of it?

A burst of clapping announced that some important event had taken place.

"That's another wicket down," said Mr. Fairfax with satisfaction. "Their second opener gone. Eighty for five. At this rate we'll have them all out by tea, and with any luck for not much more than a hundred. Better than last year. They declared at one hundred eighty for five and had us out for seventy."

"A major catastrophe," agreed Ben Sacher gravely.

The young man said something. Sacher swung round to look and then said to Mr. Fairfax, "Did anyone know that I was intending to come down here this afternoon?"

"It was a surprise for all of us."

"Then what are the press doing here?"

"The press?"

"That man with a camera."

"Where? Oh, that's all right. That's not the press. That's one of our staff. I'll introduce him."

Mr. Diplock shambled up, watched suspiciously by the young man, and shook hands with Sacher, who said, "That's a fine camera you have. You take a lot of photographs?"

"It's a Swedish Hasselblad. I've had some excellent pictures with it."

Sacher thought for a moment, and said, "Yes. I have seen one of them. Jared brought it home. It was a picture of him. He seemed to be puzzling over something. He had no idea that he was being photographed, I think."

"Actually," said Mr. Diplock, "he was trying to digest the binomial theory."

Sacher smiled suddenly, a smile that lit his face from the inside. He said, "It certainly looked as if he was trying to digest something. I thought it was a doughnut that had gone down the wrong way."

"Come and meet some of the parents," said Mr. Fairfax.

"So *you* had the police in, too," said Mrs. Paxton. "I'd no idea you had a *place* in this area. I imagined you lived in London."

"We do," said Sonia Warlock. "We took this house for the summer. Peter's in two of the four plays at the Chichester Festival this year."

"Of course. I'd forgotten."

"It was a sergeant and another man. They were very polite, but goodness, were they thorough!"

"So they were with us. They looked absolutely everywhere. No, thank you. I don't think I could manage another. They're quite delicious."

A small, stout man, who turned out to be Mr. Gedge, said, "What beats me is how they know what to look for."

"My husband says it's the scientists," said Mrs. Paxton. "They've got wonderful machines. Give them a fragment of metal or a flake of paint and they can reconstruct the whole car."

The marquee was bulging at the seams. At one end Lucy presided behind a line of trestle tables with urns of hot brown water masquerading as tea. The St. Catherine's eleven had been shepherded into one corner, where the master in charge, a young clergyman, was keeping a strict eye on them. Though it was not clear, as Nigel remarked to G.G., whether he was doing it to prevent them from being contaminated by Protestant doctrine or lured into overeating.

Ben Sacher, accompanied now by both young men, was holding court in one corner. The other guests, as tends to happen when a real celebrity is present, were divided between those who wanted to be seen talking to him, and those who were determined not to be impressed and kept as far away as possible.

The boys were scurrying round with plates of cakes and sandwiches and bowls of strawberries, smiling shyly and eating more than anyone would have thought possible.

Two of the steadiest eaters were Roger and Billy Warlock.

"If you eat one more sandwich," said McMurtrie, "you won't be able to stand up straight. Let alone bat."

"It's perfectly all right," said Roger. "Dad always says eat as much as you like before you go in to bat, *but don't drink anything.*"

"Why on earth not?"

"He was playing for the Taverners last summer. It was a match against the Middlesex Club and ground. They're jolly hot stuff, and he didn't expect to be in for more than a couple of overs. He'd been putting back pints and pints of beer. Actually, he was in rather good form. He was batting for an hour and a half. The last half hour was absolute *agony.*"

"What did he do?"

"In the end, he couldn't stand it any longer. There was only one thing to do."

"You don't mean to say . . ."

"He hit his own wicket."

Billy said, "See if you can get us another lot of strawberries. Young Cracknell has got a trayful of them."

"If you don't catch him quickly," said Roger, "there won't be any left. He's had three lots himself already. Greedy little beast."

The amount they had eaten at tea did not seem to have affected the batting ability of the Warlock twins. The St. Catherine's opener was fast for a schoolboy and bowled to an intimidating assembly of two slips, a gully and a third man. Since the first four balls of the over were shortish and on the offside, his plan was evidently to bowl for catches.

Roger made no attempt to play any of them.

This disconcerted the bowler. The fifth ball was straight and to a good length, and Roger blocked it. The last ball of the over was straight but short, and he smacked it round through the empty leg-side field for an easy four. Billy treated the slow bowler at the other end with a similar mixture of caution and contempt. Nigel breathed a sigh of relief and settled back on his heels to watch them knock off the hundred and twenty runs that were needed for victory.

At thirty they were getting into their stride. At forty the Catherine's captain had a word with the master who was umpiring at one end, and two new bowlers were brought on. The result of this was to increase the rate of the scoring.

"I used to grudge all the time they spent away from home," said Sonia Warlock. "But it almost seems worth it, doesn't it?"

"Splendid little batsmen," said Colonel Brabazon.

The boys who had not qualified for tea in the marquee were now trooping back onto the field. Commander Gaze, who was master on duty, came with them. He said to Mr. Diplock, "Have you got any idea where Manifold is? I wanted him to stand in for me for half an hour."

"Haven't seen him all afternoon," said Mr. Diplock. He was busy adjusting the telescopic lens of one of his cameras, which was fixed up on a tripod. He said, "If that fat oaf who thinks he's fielding at point would move half a step to the right, I could get just the picture I want."

"If he doesn't move back a bit," said the Commander, "Roger will decapitate him. He really is clouting them, isn't he?"

At this moment Roger executed a ringing square cut, the boy at point jumped back, and Mr. Diplock's camera clicked.

"Eighty up," said Mr. Fairfax. "I do believe we shall do it."

"Aren't you going to bat at all?" said Ben Sacher to his son.

"Not if I don't have to," said Jared. "I'd much rather watch Roger and Billy. If they'll put the hundred up, I reckon the rest of us could manage the twenty."

The score was two short of the hundred when Roger skied a

ball over the bowler's head. The St. Catherine's captain, standing almost on the boundary, caught it comfortably and Roger returned to the pavilion, removing his cap politely in acknowledgment of the applause.

Two minutes and two runs later, his twin had joined him.

"It looks as if I shall have to get my pads on after all," said Jared.

This unexpected success had clearly heartened the St. Catherine's attack. The opening bowlers came on again and in twenty painful minutes captured seven more wickets for seventeen runs.

McMurtrie, who had gone in number six, was stolidly holding up his end. He was not a great batsman, but he wasn't afraid of the fast bowler. Following Roger's example, he ignored anything on the off and presented a bat like a barn door to anything that was straight.

The last man in was Monty Gedge. He was less worried than his father, who was moist with excitement and hoarse with good advice.

"I've never made any runs in a match before," said Monty placidly, "so no one's going to be disappointed if I don't make any now, are they?"

Following the same tactics as McMurtrie, he survived the rest of the over without difficulty. The next over produced two byes.

It was a moment when good nerves were more valuable than technique. And it was the St. Catherine's fast bowler who lost his head. Trying to produce a particularly vicious ball, he overstepped the crease by a clear foot. Nigel bellowed, "No ball." McMurtrie, seeing his chance, jumped out and smote it. It was not a classic shot, but it cleared midwicket and was worth two runs. The school roared its approval. A move was made to chair the heroes back to the pavilion, but the thought of carrying McMurtrie and Gedge, both substantial characters, for fifty yards proved a deterrent. However, everyone who could get near them either patted them on the back or shook them by the hand, or managed to grab some part of their clothing.

"Like being touched for the king's evil," said Mr. Diplock.

"If it was soccer," said the Commander, "I suppose they'd be kissing them."

"Keep the boys off the pitch," said Mr. Fairfax. "We've got two more matches to play on it this term."

Colonel Brabazon said, "Splendid match. Splendid match. Very close finish. Couldn't have been better."

"I don't really understand the technique of the game," said Ben Sacher, "but it appears to me to have much in common with warfare. If you maintain your positions long enough, the other side defeats itself."

When McMurtrie got through the crowd and reached the steps of the pavilion, he received a surprise which had an element of shock in it. Sitting on a seat in front of the scorer's box, smoking a pipe and looking sunburned and relaxed, was his father.

"I've explained the situation as we see it," said Sir Charles McMurtrie. "You've got a responsibility for all your boys. Not just for one of them. The final decision must rest with you. But if I might use a metaphor which seems particularly appropriate after this afternoon, we shall have a great deal more chance of winning if we play this fixture on our own ground. You follow me?"

Mr. Fairfax nodded. He was afraid that if he said anything at all his voice would run up into a squeak and sound silly. He was desperately disturbed.

Sir Charles said, "You've got to appreciate that we're not up against people with unlimited resources. I should have said that the PFO never, at any time, had more than half a dozen agents who could operate with impunity in this country. This is *not* their home ground. They can buy a certain amount of help, through criminal contacts, but such people are subordinates. People who drive cars and do a bit of shooting. They're not organizers, and they're not principals. As I said, you could almost count those on the fingers of one hand." He paused for a moment and added,

"And we got three of them in the embassy job."

"Then what you're telling me," said Mr. Fairfax, speaking very carefully, "is that there are only one or two left in this country who are really dangerous."

"At the moment, and for some time to come. Yes."

Speaking of it like that, in the calm of a beautiful summer evening, with the square and reassuring figure of Sir Charles McMurtrie filling his visitor's chair, it suddenly seemed to be rather less alarming.

"You can't be sure that they'll try."

"Certainly not. You may have a very peaceful remainder of the term. I hope you will. If you were to send young Sacher away, of course, you'd be perfectly safe."

Mr. Fairfax had made up his mind. He was afraid that if he thought about it much longer he would say no. He said, "I'll have a word with Sacher. If he agrees that his son should stay on for the rest of this term, I shan't ask him to take him away."

Sir Charles said, "You can rest assured that I, and quite a number of other people, will be doing our best to see that you don't run into any trouble. Would it be all right if Alastair came out with me now? I'll take him to dinner somewhere and return him by nine o'clock."

"Certainly." When his visitor was at the door, he added, "He's a very balanced boy. One of the best all-rounders I've ever had anything to do with."

"You must take some credit for that," said Sir Charles.

"I can only put it in this way," said Ben Sacher. "The security forces of this country, for whom I have considerable respect, are convinced that one further move has already been planned against me. In the future, no doubt, there will be others. Any servant of the Israeli state who lives or moves abroad is a target. But evil, like good, takes time to mature. You follow me?"

"Yes," said Mr. Fairfax. His mind was made up. He simply wished that people would stop talking about it.

"There are indications, from certain preliminary moves which have been noted, that the blow may fall here. We have, of course, no right to place you or your staff or the boys under your charge in any sort of danger."

"No," said Mr. Fairfax.

"Although one might argue"—as Sacher said this, for the second time that day a smile lit up his face—"that since in the present state of the world no boy is likely to go through the whole of his life without meeting violence in some form or other, it would be part of a good preparatory school curriculum to prepare him for it. In the same way, I believe, that you encourage boys to get over mumps and measles at this stage in their lives, when they can absorb the result more easily. However, that is not perhaps an analogy which I should press too far."

"If such an attempt were made," said Mr. Fairfax abruptly, "the only person in any immediate danger would be your son?"

"That is correct. If everyone does what he is told to do and keeps his head, there should be no danger to anyone else."

"And you are prepared to accept the responsibility for that? The danger to him?"

"There is no question of my accepting responsibility by proxy. Jared is of age to accept it for himself. In your religion you call it the age of confirmation. We call it bar mitzvah. Jared will make up his own mind. I shall not make it up for him."

"You can call it what you like," said Mr. Fairfax testily. "He's still a boy. You could take him away, if you wished. There are plenty of places you could hide him for the time being."

"Yes," said Sacher. "He could hide. For the time being. But there is a drawback. If you run away the first time you see danger, it is twice as easy to run away the second time. And when you have started running, it is very difficult to stop. But I am only telling you something your own father must often have told you."

For the first time in this remarkable conversation, Mr. Fairfax was really surprised.

"You knew my father?" he said.

"It was in the days of the mandate. Your father had command of one of the brigades in the occupation force. I was, of course, only a boy at the time. I had a very small part in the blowing up of his car."

Sir Charles McMurtrie and his son dined together in candlelit luxury at the Bon Pastor Hotel. With the coffee Sir Charles ordered a large glass of port for himself and a small one for his son and said, "Were you surprised to see me?"

"Seeing it's only the second time in six years that you've been down," said Alastair, "yes."

"You haven't asked me why I've come."

"I thought it was to watch me play cricket."

"Partly," said his father. "But only partly. Actually I've come to give you some instructions. They are the sort of instructions which had to be given personally. I thought I'd keep them until after dinner. I didn't want to risk spoiling your appetite."

"Thank you," said Alastair faintly.

"The first thing I have to tell you is to stop whatever inquiries you think you're making about Mr. Manifold."

The candlelight spared Alastair's blushes. He said, "I suppose Miss Lindsay told you."

"Miss Lindsay is well aware of who Mr. Manifold is, and what he is doing. And that brings me to my second point. Sometime —I can't tell you when, but before the end of term—he may give you an order. It might happen at any time. And it will be a simple order, like 'Get up' or 'Sit quite still' or possibly 'Fall down.' Something like that."

"Would it just be me?"

"It might be you, or Peter Joscelyne, but more probably Jared. So pass it on to them. But no one else. You're to be on the alert, all three of you. *Because when you get that order, wherever you are, and whatever you're doing, you're to obey it at once.*"

12

Andrew Pickering, the chief constable of Surrey, was not a retired soldier or sailor. He was a policeman, who had climbed every rung on the ladder to reach his present position. This made him both more and less difficult for a visiting chief superintendent like Jock Anderson to deal with.

More difficult because he was unlikely to be bluffed. Easier because the two men spoke the same language.

Pickering said, "Superintendent Oldham has passed up to me the record of the Disciplinary Board on Sergeant Callaghan. On the main count, there's no question that he was in the wrong. He neglected to take the proper procedures laid down on receipt of the order 'Huntsman.' He should have telephoned you at once, himself. The procedures had been explained to him. He understood them. He failed to carry them out, *even when his own superintendent had given him the word.*"

"He's not a young man. And it was an awkward time of night."

"Those are reasons. Not excuses. Some penalty will have to be imposed. But my real point is a different one. If we make an example of Callaghan, the object of the exercise, as I see it, will be to make sure that this particular lapse doesn't occur again. Right?"

"I don't want Sergeant Callaghan crucified," said Anderson. "It was just that, by luck, we did have a real chance of catching this man. It may never happen just like that again."

"That's the point I wanted to be clear about," said Pickering. "You think that if you'd been alerted soon after half-past eleven, instead of some hours later, you really would have been able to put your hand on this man. He'd have had more than an hour's start. A car can go a long way in an hour."

"Agreed. But I don't think he'd have got clear of the net I should have been able to spread." He took a map out of his briefcase and unfolded it on the table. He said, "I started organizing this in a small way after the first case and elaborated it after the second one. Each of those blue crosses is a watcher or a potential watcher."

Pickering said, "I didn't know we had that number of resident policemen."

"They're not policemen. Although some of them are retired policemen. They are A.A. and R.A.C. scouts, railway linesmen and level-crossing keepers, night watchmen, midwives, game-keepers, retired people who don't go to bed too early and insomniacs who don't go to bed at all. One of the most reliable is an amateur astronomer. Another is a radio ham who finds he gets his best transmissions between midnight and three in the morning. They are all on the telephone, or can be reached very quickly by a telephone call. Within five minutes of being alerted I can have a hundred people on watch."

"And they have authority to stop cars?"

"Certainly not. Their job is simply to note the make and number of *any* car which passes. A lot of them, as you see, live on crossroads. When their reports have been collated, I doubt if a single car could move, by night, across that particular area without our being able to say, within a quarter of a mile, where it came from and where it went to. I had a trial run last month."

"Successful?"

"Most successful. I think that one high court judge would be very embarrassed if we were to publish our conclusions on where *he* went that night."

Pickering was studying the map with fascination. He said, "Did you know that I lived in this area?"

"No, sir."

"What night did you run this trial?"

"It was May twenty-second. Just three weeks before the Lister case."

The chief constable seemed to be making a calculation. Then he said, "No. It's all right. I was in Blackpool at a chief constables' conference."

Both men laughed.

"Seriously, though," said Pickering, "you think this would have picked him up? Suppose he lived outside the area?"

"I don't think he does. But if he had run off the edge, we should have extended the network in that direction and tracked him to earth next time. After all, even without using this method, we succeeded in tracing the car a fair distance. You've seen my report."

"Yes," said Pickering. "Fred showed it to me." He was still fascinated by the little crosses on the map. "Did you invent this yourself?"

"I read about it," said Anderson. "It's the method the French used during the war to keep track of the movements of Gestapo officers and collaborators and other undesirable characters. They called it *Le Réseau des Yeux.* The Network of Eyes. It was very effective."

Jock Anderson had another meeting that afternoon. It was a repeat of the conference on the previous Monday with the representatives of the four county forces. Reports from the hundreds of men involved had been carefully tabulated. The fact that the results so far were negative did not disturb them. They knew that, in the mathematics of police work, a thousand negatives might add up to one positive.

"We ran a check," said Anderson, "with the motor licensing authorities and compiled a list of all cars from addresses in the search area of this particular type which had their licenses renewed during the past twelve months. And we have visited all the owners. In every case we were able to eliminate the cars concerned."

"And your conclusions?" said Colonel Brabazon.

"It confirms what I had thought all along, sir. This man has two cars. One he goes about his business in. The other he keeps under cover somewhere and uses only when he's out on the prowl."

"Might be one he's stolen," said Woolmer.

"Could be," said Anderson. "But on balance I think not. He's not a professional car thief."

"I agree," said the colonel. "Most likely it will turn out to be an old car. One he'd hoped to sell when he bought a new one and then he couldn't dispose of it. He tucked it away somewhere, but hasn't bothered to license it."

"Something like that, I think," said Anderson. They were all silent for a moment. They had thought about that car a lot. Anderson sometimes dreamed about it. He was walking through a thick wood and came on a clearing. In the clearing was a hut. And in the hut was an old dark-gray car. He usually woke up before he could write the number down.

"Those shaded areas, on the large-scale map," he said, "are the ones we've gone over thoroughly." The shading, they could see, formed a wide crescent moving toward Chichester, spreading its wings twenty-five miles in either direction.

"We've alerted every garage and motor dealer in the southeast. If anyone gets a tire changed or asks for a respray, we hear about it at once."

"He wouldn't be so daft," said Lowry.

"What would you do, Fred, if it was your car?"

"No use trying to burn it," said Woolmer. "We'd hear about that, too."

"Even if you took off the plates, burning wouldn't destroy the engine number and gearbox number."

"You're asking me what I'd do," said Lowry. "So I'll tell you. You say I've got two cars. One I use, and the other I've got under cover. And if the second car's found it could be traced back to me. Right?"

"That's the assumption we're working on," said Anderson.

"Then I'll tell you what I'd do. I'd take that second car to pieces, nut by nut and bolt by bolt. And I'd put the pieces in my other car and I'd run out by night and dump them in the deepest, loneliest gullies I could find. Not all in the same place. A head-light here, a wheel there. Finding one or two bits wouldn't help you. You'd need to put the car together again to prove it was mine."

"It'd take you some time," said Anderson.

"You'd need more than time," said Woolmer. "You'd need a complete workshop. A car doesn't take to pieces like a clockwork toy. You'd have to saw up the paneling. It'd be a hell of a job."

"It would be a noisy job," said Colonel Brabazon. "And that brings us to the main point we have to decide. Do we broadcast or not? It's a close decision. What we're trying to do is to panic this man, make him do something silly. We haven't succeeded yet. If he'd made any obvious efforts to dispose of the car or disguise it, I'm sure we should have heard of it. That means that wherever the car's hidden, he's satisfied that it's reasonably safe. He's kept his nerve."

"So far," said Anderson.

"I agree. He's probably getting close to the breaking point. He knows we're closing in on him. If we broadcast a full description of the car, with an explanation of why we're looking for it, that won't tell him anything he doesn't know already. But it will alert his neighbors. One of them remembers: Didn't so-and-so have an old car? He was going to sell it, but he never did. Funny thing, we haven't seen it about lately."

"Or he hears a lot of hammering by night," said Woolmer.

"I think the arguments in favor are stronger than those against," said the colonel. He looked round the table. There was no dissent. He said, "It will take a little arranging. And I want to complete the preliminary search. We'll ask the BBC to put it out after the news next Monday, and repeat it every night during the week."

Old Mr. Moritz, Rosie's grandfather, had reached an age when he moved slowly and thought slowly. His life ran on comfortable lines. He rose late, looked through the daily paper his daughter bought for him. It had more pictures in it than print, which suited Mr. Moritz, who had never been a great reader. He usually had a sleep in the afternoon, listened to the six o'clock news, and enjoyed his tea, the main meal of his day. After tea, when the weather was fine, he pottered down the half mile of road that separated No. 2 Jubilee Cottages from the village of Brading and the Three Horseshoes, which was his objective.

When he passed the entrance to farmer Laycock's field he used to think about that night, now nearly a month in the past, and of the things that had happened. He thought about Rosie, who seemed to have gone off Des Maybury. Old Mr. Moritz was no fool. He knew right enough what they'd been up to in that field. Five minutes more, and Des would have had what he wanted from her. When he was a youngster, an escapade like that would have meant marriage. Now she was probably on the pill, the little slut.

He thought about the boy. The one they'd found in the field. He'd forgotten his name, but he remembered the details of what had been done to him. Horrible things, but somehow exciting, too. And he remembered his own part in it. He'd been interviewed a lot by the police and the press. After all, he'd been the one who had seen the car come out and drive away.

Drive away.

For the hundredth time, a recollection flickered through old Mr. Moritz's brain. It was as faint and as fleeting as the flicker of light on a radar screen; no sooner seen than gone. But coming back again and again with irritating persistence.

He was certain that he had noticed something. Something that might be of great importance. Something that he certainly ought to report, if only he could remember what it was. It was something he had noticed when the car was going away from him. Not when it was coming out, and had nearly knocked him down, but when it was driving away down the road.

It had been dusk, the dusk of a fine day near to midsummer. That was how he was able to see something of the car when it came rushing out, seeming to come straight for him, then went into a skidding turn at the last moment and accelerated off up the darkening road toward the village. If it had been properly dark, he wouldn't have been able to see anything at all. He wouldn't have been able to give the police all those details about the color and shape of the car.

Not that they had been grateful. They seemed to think that he ought to have noticed the make and the number. As if anyone, at a moment like that, would have been likely to notice the number. And anyway, it would have been too dark to see it.

The thoughts in Mr. Moritz's head were apt to go round in a circle. It was getting dark, so the car lights should have been on. But the headlights and side lights weren't on. That was the first thing he'd noticed about the car. Silly fool, driving without lights on. And yet he had a feeling that the rear lights had been on. No difficulty about that. The man might have switched them on as he drove away. So what was worrying him?

Mr. Moritz shook his head angrily and stumped off down the road, one vital piece of information, which the police would have given their right hands to possess, still locked in his muddled old brain.

13

The car had come by a roundabout route along small roads to the west of Tinmans Common. As it approached the side gate of Trenchard House, the driver turned off all the lights and killed the engine, and the car slid through the darkness and came to rest a few yards past the gate.

After that, for a long time nothing happened.

There were two men in the car besides the driver. All sat quite still. When the clock of Boxwood church chimed out the hour of two, it seemed to act as some sort of signal. The man beside the driver opened the car door and stepped out. He could now be seen to be very tall and thin, and to be carrying a pair of metal shears, with stubby blades and long handles.

The chain that circled the gatepost and the nearest upright of the gate was fastened by a padlock. The man took two lengths of black cord from his pocket and with them lashed the chain firmly to both gatepost and gate. Then he centered the blades of the shears on the small length of chain between the cords and exerted his full strength and leverage on the handles.

There was a single sharp snap as the metal jaws bit home. The man laid the shears down, undid the right-hand cord and slipped the severed end of the chain through the now useless padlock. Then he opened the gate, lifting it clear of the ground so that it made no noise. While this had been going on, the man in the back of the car had got out and was watching toward the main road.

Both men now went round to the front of the car and, with the driver steering, pushed it in reverse through the gate. They stationed it under the shadow of the cedar tree, took out two army blankets and covered the whole of the hood and windshield. When this had been done, the tall man shut the gate, slipped the padlock back into position and retied the loose end of the chain. Anyone passing down the road would have needed to examine the chain carefully to notice that there was anything amiss; and he would have needed night sight as good as that of the owl— who was observing these maneuvers with interest—to have spotted the car under the deep shadow of the tree.

The quarter sounded from the church clock.

The tall man and his companion set off, making a circuit of the lawn, keeping in the shadow of the trees, until they reached the end of the west wing of the house. The third window they tried was unlatched. They lifted the sash and climbed through. The eye of a pencil flashlight, illuminating the blackboard, showed them that they were in a classroom. They opened the door softly and stepped out into the passage.

At the end of the passage the tall man used his light again. First he unbolted and unlocked the side door. Then he set off up the staircase. He moved with the certainty of a man who knew exactly where he was going and what he was going to do.

Alastair McMurtrie sat up in bed. Something had jerked him out of a shallow, dream-haunted sleep. It took him two seconds to realize what had woken him. The creak of the board at the end of the passage outside.

His watch was on the table beside his bed. He rolled over and saw that it was nearly half-past two. Could the masters have resumed their sentry go? If so, why? And which of them was it? These thoughts were in his head when the door opened and the two men came in.

A light shone straight at him. From behind the light the tall man said, quite pleasantly, "So you're awake, are you, boy? Then you can do something for me. Get out of bed, very quietly, and wake up young Sacher."

"Why—"

"Do what you're told, and maybe you won't get hurt."

The light had been switched off, and in the moonlight he could see the men quite clearly. A recollection of what his father had said came back to him. He climbed out of bed and went across to Sacher. As soon as he got there he could see that he, too, was awake. He bent over and made a show of shaking his arm.

Jared sat up and said, "What's up? What is it?"

"These men say you've got to get up."

"All right," said the tall man. "I'll take over now. Out of bed, young fellow. And get some clothes on. You're coming with us."

Sacher started to say something and then stopped. The flashlight had been shifted to the man's left hand. The right hand now held a gun, capped with a bulbous silencer, very like the one they had seen in Mr. Manifold's drawer.

"Just to get things clear straightaway," said the tall man. "If you don't do what I tell you quickly and quietly, I'm going to shoot one of your young friends in the guts. You understand me?"

Sacher nodded. His mouth was dry and his heart was thumping. He was afraid to trust his voice.

"I'll give you one minute to get dressed. Sweater and trousers will be enough. Put them on over your pajamas. Then slippers. Don't bother about shoes and socks."

While Sacher was shuffling into his clothes, McMurtrie shot a quick look at the second man. He was at the far side of the window, looking out. From where he stood he commanded a view of the lawn and the front drive and could see the top but not the foot of the cedar tree. It was noticeable that he had not allowed anything that was going on in the room to distract his attention.

The tall man said to McMurtrie, "One more word. When we leave, don't do anything silly like running out after us. There's a third man outside, round the turn of the stairs. He'll be there

122

covering us for exactly five minutes. If you try to follow us, he'll shoot your legs off. Understood?"

McMurtrie nodded. The man turned to Joscelyne, who was sitting up in bed, silent and staring. "You, too."

Joscelyne said, "I understand."

"All right. You've behaved very sensibly so far. Keep it up. . . . All clear outside?"

The second man said, "I thought I saw a light, two minutes ago, up by the main gate, where the patrol car stops. Nothing this end."

"All right," said the tall man. "Let's go."

Then the light came on.

It was Latrobe, standing in the doorway. He was wearing a dressing gown, his hair was on end and his eyes were still sticky with sleep.

He said, "What on earth . . . ?"

The tall man said, "Get out of the way, or collect a bullet."

Latrobe took in the fact that Sacher was dressed, and that the tall man was holding him by one arm. He said, "Leave him alone. Leave him alone at once," and hurled himself straight at the gun.

The tall man took a step to one side, lifted the gun and cracked Latrobe over the head with the long barrel, weighted by the silencer. Latrobe fell forward across the foot of Sacher's bed and the second man turned out the light.

The interlude had lasted five seconds.

The tall man said, "Just remember what I told you."

Then they were gone. The board at the end of the passage creaked. Then silence.

McMurtrie said, speaking in a whisper, "We've got to get help. Connie may be bleeding to death."

"They'll shoot us if we go out."

"I think that was rot. They always say something like that just to stop you from following. Come on."

The two boys tiptoed down the passage and peered round the corner of the stairs. There was no one there. They cascaded down both flights and out into the main hall. On a table by the front door stood the school bell. McMurtrie seized it in both hands and started to ring it vigorously.

Mr. Fairfax was the first to arrive. He listened to what McMurtrie had to say and ran for the telephone in his study. It took him a few seconds to realize that it wasn't working. By the time he got back into the hall most of the school seemed to be there. He shouted above the babble of voices, "No one is to go outside the building. See to it Warr. Come with me, Commander."

He unbolted the front door and went out. The moon shone down coldly on an empty space of gravel. Mr. Fairfax said, "The telephone's been put out of action. The quickest way to get help will be to get hold of the police car at the main gate."

"Right," said the Commander. He doubled off up the front drive.

Mr. Fairfax stood on the steps, looking after him. He felt that there were things that he ought to be doing, steps to be taken. A thought occurred to him. Where was Sergeant Baker? And where, for that matter, was Manifold? The two men who should have been most useful in a crisis seemed to have disappeared.

He went back into the house. Mr. Diplock had now appeared. And Lucy was there, listening to McMurtrie repeat his story for the third time. She said, "I'd better go up and look after Connie. If he's really bad, one of the policemen will have to fetch Dr. Baines."

Mr. Fairfax said, "All boys back to bed. At once. Would you see to it, please, Warr. Anyone I find out of bed in one minute I will deal with myself."

Reluctantly the boys began to disperse.

"McMurtrie and Joscelyne, you'd better stay. The police will want to talk to you."

"If they don't put on a few more clothes," said Mr. Diplock, who was himself wearing a heavy dressing gown, a scarf and a pair of plaid slippers, "they'll be catching very serious colds. The night air is far from warm."

"Yes. Run up and get on your dressing gowns. But hurry."

By the time the boys came down, the police car was at the door. The sergeant in charge was talking on the wireless. The conversation seemed to go on interminably. (Hurry, hurry, thought McMurtrie. Poor Jared, bound and blindfolded, his mouth gagged with sticking plaster, bundled into the back of a car.)

The sergeant withdrew his head from the window of the car and said, "That should be all right, sir. We had three lots of roadblocks set up. They've all been alerted. They'll be lucky if they get past."

"Suppose they leave the car and strike across country?"

"They could do that, sir. But I don't think they'd get very far. This looks like the top brass. They'll want to hear it from the boys, I expect."

Two more cars came racing up the drive. Colonel Brabazon was in the front one. He jumped out, had a quick word with the sergeant, listened to McMurtrie's account and said to Mr. Fairfax, "Have you told the boy's father?"

"I couldn't. The telephone's dead."

"We shall have to let him know. I'll send the second car back." He had been joined by Superintendent Barclay from Chichester. "There's a lot to do. If they get through the roadblocks we'll have to put out an all-stations alert. Ten to one they'll be making for London."

(A house in the docks, thought McMurtrie. A damp cellar. Rats.)

As the superintendent strode off to give orders to the second car, Lucy Fairfax appeared at the top of the steps. Latrobe was standing beside her, a gaunt Turk, his head turbaned in bandages. "Silly man," said Lucy. "I told him to go to bed, but he would come down."

Latrobe grabbed hold of Mr. Fairfax by the arm and said, almost fiercely, "What have they done to him? Did they get away? I tried to stop them."

"You did your best," said Mr. Fairfax. "I'm sorry that we

weren't all as alert as you were. . . ." He felt Latrobe stiffen, and thought for a moment that he was going to pass out. Then he saw that he was staring at something, and turned his head to see what it was.

Jared Sacher was coming toward them. His face was the color of paper, and he was walking like someone asleep.

There was a moment of paralyzed silence. Then Latrobe pushed past Mr. Fairfax, rushed up to Jared and seized him by the arm as if to convince himself that the boy was real.

He said, in a voice which excitement and emotion had pushed up almost into the treble key, "What happened, Jared? Where are those men? How did you get away? Thank God you're safe."

Jared turned his head slowly, as if uncertain where the questions were coming from. Then he said, quietly but quite clearly, "They let me go," and folded forward. Latrobe got one arm under him as he fell and straightened up, lifting the boy in his arms.

(For a long time afterward, McMurtrie had only to close his eyes and he could see the whole scene, etched in black and white under the waning moon. On the steps, the Commander with his mouth open and his teeth showing. Beside him, Mr. Diplock with his eyes half closed, as though he were visualizing the scene through the eye of a camera. The background ring of policemen, standing like dark images. And in the middle, Latrobe holding the boy in his arms.)

For a moment, no one seemed to know what to do next. It was Lucy Fairfax who moved. She said, "He's suffering from shock. Bring him in at once. He ought to be kept warm. I'll make up a bed for him in the spare room."

The scene dissolved, and broke. Latrobe followed her up the front steps, carrying Jared. Colonel Brabazon said, "As soon as he's fit to talk, you know, we ought to hear what he has to say."

Manifold said, "If he really is suffering from shock, he ought to be given a sedative. Not asked a lot of questions."

(And where had *he* come from? McMurtrie wondered. He

126

could swear that he hadn't been there a moment before.)

"You may be right," said the colonel. "Mustn't take any chances. Be thankful we've got the boy back in one piece, eh?"

He seemed to be talking at Manifold, who said, "Yes, indeed, sir. That's the main point, isn't it?"

"All the same, better leave a man behind. He needn't sit in the boy's room, but he ought to be on hand to take a statement just as soon as he's fit to talk. Would you organize that, Superintendent?"

"I'll deal with you in the morning," said Mr. Fairfax. This was to half a dozen bold spirits who had crept down into the back of the hall to see what crumbs of excitement they could pick up. "Take their names, would you, Commander. And get back to your beds *at once*. You, too, Joscelyne and McMurtrie."

McMurtrie was yawning uncontrollably. He could not remember ever feeling so tired.

14

"The Greek mathematician Pythagoras," said Mr. Diplock, "was the first to establish, largely by methods of trial and error, that the square of the hypotenuse of a right-angled triangle must be equal to the sum of the squares of the other two sides. We are able to demonstrate this great truth by a simple construction. Thus, I draw a right-angled triangle, ABC. I then construct squares on each of its three sides—"

"Sir."

"Yes, Paxton?"

"Is this the window they came through?"

"I understand that it was found open in the morning."

"Then this *was* the room."

"I imagine so."

"Goodness!"

One-A gazed round the room. No longer an ordinary classroom. A room through which would-be kidnappers had come during the night.

"I saw Jared this morning, sir," said McMurtrie. "After Dr. Baines had been. He was having his breakfast in bed. Two boiled eggs."

"I think it was a put-up job," said Roger Warlock. "I don't believe he was suffering from shock at all."

"Unless it was the shock of finding himself in Connie's arms," suggested Joscelyne.

"*What* did you say, Joscelyne?"

"I said, sir, that it must have been an awful shock. I'm glad he didn't come to any harm."

"I don't believe you said that," said Mr. Diplock. "I believe you made a very impertinent remark about a member of the staff."

"Don't you think, sir," said McMurtrie, "that Connie—I mean Mr. Latrobe—behaved like a hero?"

"Hero," said Mr. Diplock, "is one of the most misused words in the English language. To the Greeks it signified a man of high position who was faced with a critical choice, imposed on him by the Fates, or by some contradiction in his own character. Where he made the wrong decision, the result was tragedy. The revolting journalistic practice of today has cheapened the word until it means—hah!—a professional footballer who scores the odd goal in three in a cup tie."

McMurtrie, who was perfectly well aware that any mention of the word "hero" was calculated to inflame Mr. Diplock, had inserted his comment solely in order to divert the lightning from Joscelyne.

"G.G. did his bit as well," said Paxton. "I shouldn't have cared to run down that drive. He might have been shot at."

One-A considered the matter. They felt that a certain amount of credit must be allowed to the Commander. A mention in dispatches possibly. The Victoria Cross had to go to Connie, who had appeared at breakfast that morning with a most impressive band of adhesive plaster across the back of his head.

"What I want to know," said Billy Warlock, "is where was Sergeant Baker? I thought he was meant to be looking after Jared."

"Asleep."

"My father says," said Gedge, "that beer drinkers sleep very soundly."

"He ought to know," said Paxton.

"Beer's a healthier drink than whisky, isn't it, sir?"

"Since I drink neither whisky nor beer, Gedge," said Mr. Diplock, "I am unable to offer any opinion on the subject. You will note that I have constructed a square on the hypotenuse, AC. We then drop a perpendicular from B to cut the base of the square ACPQ at X."

"T.E.F. beat *five* boys this morning," said Billy Warlock. "Cracknell, Hills, Gould, Stokes and Walkinshaw. They got four each."

"Serve them right," said Paxton. "Silly asses. There was no point in going downstairs. They could have seen it all from the window, like we did."

Mr. Diplock drew a small book from his pocket. He said, "The next boy who talks will receive a double demerit. Since the headmaster appears to be in a flagellatory mood this morning, no doubt he will take the hint. You understand me? Good. We now join points B and Q and consider triangle ABQ, which lies, as you will observe, between the parallel lines AQ and BX. . . ."

"I told Dr. Baines," said Lucy, "that I would accept no responsibility. What Jared needs is a complete rest. *Not* a lot of people bothering him with questions."

"And what did the learned Dr. Baines say to that?" said Elizabeth.

"He said he thought the boy would be easier when he'd got the story off his chest."

"He looked perfectly easy when I took him up his breakfast this morning. And he ate it all."

"You always have to be careful with shock."

"People talk more nonsense about shock," said Elizabeth, "than any other word in the medical vocabulary. It isn't something your maiden aunt suffers from when she sees the dog from next door demonstrating the facts of life to her bitch. It's a simple defense mechanism, switched on by the body in time of stress."

"Of course," said Lucy coldly. "I'd forgotten. You must know a good deal about shock. You once worked in a loony bin, didn't you?"

"The correct description," said Elizabeth, "is simply 'hospital.'

Or in some cases 'mental hospital.' I suppose it's living in a place like this that makes you use infantile expressions like 'loony bin.' "

Lucy looked at Elizabeth sharply. She said, "That sounded to me very like impertinence."

"You have excellent hearing," said Elizabeth. "It *was* impertinence."

"In that case—"

"In that case," said Elizabeth, "you will be forced to suggest to your husband that my employment here should be terminated. Spare yourself the trouble. We're going."

"Oh? When?"

"At the end of term. We're planning to get married in August."

"By 'we' I assume you mean yourself and Warr."

"You didn't think I was going to marry Mr. Diplock, did you?"

"I'm very sorry," said Mr. Fairfax. "He's an excellent all-round sportsman, and he'd brought the cricket side on tremendously."

"He's a beautiful young man," said Lucy. "And he's as soft and wet as a sponge."

"One wouldn't, perhaps, describe him as an intellectual."

"It'll be a wonderful marriage. She's as tough as whipcord and he's got no more moral fiber than a seven-year-old child. The physical side should be terrific. And of course we all know how important *that* is."

Mr. Fairfax said, with the weary patience of someone approaching a subject that had been discussed too often and too thoroughly, "If you think it would do any good, we could go back to the marriage guidance people."

"Poking you about and telling you how to lie in bed," said Lucy. "Certainly not."

"We went straight out by the side door," said Jared. "I think they must have unlocked it before they came up. It's usually shut at night."

"Very likely," said Superintendent Barclay.

There was something about the boy that puzzled him. He had certainly recovered his spirits, and that was natural enough. Boys got over things very quickly. It was the way he was dealing with his questions. He answered them readily enough. Possibly a little bit too readily, with a lot of irrelevant information thrown in each time. The superintendent spent much of his working life in law courts and had noticed witnesses who behaved like that. It didn't necessarily mean that they were lying; only that they were being very careful. The extra bit they threw in gave them time to anticipate what the next question might be.

"What happened then?"

"We walked across the lawn. I was in the middle between the two men. They were on either side of me."

"Were they holding you?"

"Yes. They had one arm each."

"And then?"

"When we got quite close to the car—it was parked under a tree—the big cedar—"

"The one near the gate into the side road?"

"That's the one. I didn't see the car until I was quite close to it. I think they'd put blankets or something over it to cover the metalwork. It was quite a bright moonlight night."

"And when you got up to the car?"

"There was a third man. I thought perhaps he might have been the driver. Or someone they'd left behind to look after the car."

"Very likely."

"Well, he was standing beside the car, leaning his head through the window, using a wireless set. At least, I think it must have been a wireless set. He had one of those things—what do you call them . . . ?"

"A hand microphone?"

"That's right. He said something into it. I couldn't hear what it was. Then he beckoned to the tall man, and they moved round to the front of the car. The other man was still holding me, and I did think I might wriggle loose and dash off into the bushes, but now he had one hand on my arm and the other one twisted into the neck of my sweater. I didn't think there was much hope. Then the tall man came back—"

"Did you hear what the driver said to him?"

"No. I don't think they wanted me to hear. They were some way away, and speaking very quietly."

"What next?"

"Then the tall man came back and said to me, 'We've had some news which has made us change our plans. You're not coming with us.' I thought he meant they were going to shoot me on the spot and I was too scared to do anything except stand there and look at him. Then he said, 'You're very lucky. If you do exactly what I tell you, you'll be all right.' So of course I said I would and he said, 'Shut your eyes and count two hundred, quite slowly. Then you can go.' As I started to count, I heard the car start and drive away."

"Was the gate open?"

For the first time there was a break in the fluency of Jared's answer. Then he said, "Well, you see, I had my eyes shut."

"You had your eyes shut," agreed the superintendent patiently. "But if the gate had been closed you'd have heard the car stop, and someone get out to open it, and the car start up again."

"Of course I should. And I didn't. So it must have been open, mustn't it?"

"That's the story the police are working on," said Manifold. "They've organized a search for the men and the car, but since Jared could give practically no description of the men, and no description at all of the car, they don't hold out much prospect of success."

"I assume," said Mr. Fairfax, "that it is also the story which the press will be told."

"If they get hold of it at all."

"I hardly see how it can be kept a secret when every boy in the school knows that something happened."

"Couldn't you tell them to keep their mouths shut?"

"I know from experience," said Mr. Fairfax, "that it would be totally ineffective. However, it's a blessing that it should have happened on a Tuesday."

"What difference does that make?"

"Boys are creatures of habit. Sunday is the only day on which letters home are written. By next Monday every parent will have a garbled account of what took place and most of them will telephone me. Some of them will inevitably spread the story. The press will pick it up."

"No newspaper's going to get excited about an attempted kidnapping which is a week old and which didn't come off."

"You may be right," said Mr. Fairfax. "I hope so." He was finding it difficult to adjust himself to the change between addressing an assistant master and a police officer. "You took a considerable chance, didn't you?"

"The object of the whole operation," said Manifold, "the one thing that really mattered, was to get the men clear of the school. Can you imagine the sort of situation which would have developed if they'd been forced to hole up inside the school with half a dozen boys as hostages?"

Mr. Fairfax shuddered and said, "Yes."

"That was the whole basis of the plan. To let them take the boy out to the car."

"How did you know where the car would be?"

"Not too difficult. If you had a lively prisoner to transport and needed to use a car to transport him in, there were only two possible approaches. The main gate and the side gate. We had a police car at the main gate, put a chain on the side gate, as well as having the perimeter patrolled from time to time. So you see, we were really offering them three choices. Leave the car a fair distance away out of sight in one of the lanes round the back end of Tinmans Common. The drawback to that is obvious. When you've got a hostage, and a slippery one at that, you want to get him into the car as quickly as possible. Second choice, park the car *outside* the side gate. Quicker for a getaway but much too dangerous. If the police patrol saw a car at that particular point they'd be bound to investigate. Third, and much the most likely alternative, cut the chain and park the car, under cover, *inside* the grounds. Shutting the gate once they were in would cause a little delay in getting away, true. But on balance it was a risk worth taking in case a patrol came past while they were doing the job and happened to look at the gate."

"It seems logical enough when you put it like that," said Mr. Fairfax.

"There was one great advantage from our point of view. When they cut the chain they signaled their arrival."

"How?"

"Wonders of science," said Manifold with a grin. "A very thin wire, almost invisible even in daylight, threaded through the chain. When they broke it, a warning sounded in Sergeant Baker's room."

Mr. Fairfax said, "I see," once more. "Well, thank God it's all over. I gathered from what the boy's father said that if you were able"—he hesitated as if looking for the appropriate word—"were able to account for these two men, no further trouble was likely to develop."

"You can set your mind at rest on that score," said Manifold. "For the time being they've shot their bolt. It's only two weeks to the end of term. Jared is quite safe here now. Incidentally, I understand that his father has canceled his entry to Winchester and is taking him back with him to finish his education in Israel."

"So he told me, when I telephoned him this morning. I thought it a pity. The boy has an exceptionally good brain."

"They do *have* schools in Israel."

"Not as good as Winchester," said Mr. Fairfax firmly. It was clear from the way he spoke that he was fast recovering his spirits. "It really has been quite a term. First Mollison's breakdown. Then the disinfestation business, and now this." Assistant masters, head lice, kidnappers. All now, happily, in the past.

A further thought struck Mr. Fairfax. "I imagine you'll be leaving us now that you've finished your work here. A pity. You had a considerable talent as a schoolmaster. I don't know what we shall do without you. I don't suppose the agencies will be able to send us anyone for two weeks."

"You may have to put up with me a bit longer," said Manifold.

"Oh?"

"You were saying just now that my work here was finished. I'm afraid that isn't true. I was glad to give Sergeant Baker a hand with looking after Sacher. But that wasn't the reason I came here."

After a moment's silence Mr. Fairfax said, "Then perhaps you'd be good enough to explain exactly what you *are* doing here."

"I expect you read in the papers about the boy, Lister, who was picked up and killed, after he'd been maltreated."

"I seem to remember it, yes."

"That was on the evening of June twelfth. The first day of your half-term break."

"I believe it was."

"It happened about thirty-five miles away from here, near a place called Brading, on the other side of Horsham. It was the third incident of its kind, and a special squad had been formed to deal with it, operating under the chief constables of the four counties concerned. Their men were on the spot pretty quickly. Not as quickly as they might have been, because of a slip-up, but quick enough to get a good look at the place before too many people had trampled over it. At the side of the track leading down to the corner of the field, between the place where the man had obviously parked his car and the hedge, they found this bit of paper. It had been folded three or four times, and from a mark on it, it was pretty clear that it had been used to wedge a rattling glass in one of the windows of the car. One of the offside windows presumably, as it had fallen off on that side."

Manifold was speaking slowly, spinning out the sentences so that he could watch Mr. Fairfax's face as he examined the small square of paper that he had unfolded and laid on his desk.

It was a black-printed demerit slip.

15

Mr. Fairfax started, twice, to say something. On the third occasion, when it came out, the overriding note was irritation.

He said, "I don't understand. What are you trying to tell me? A number of schools use devices of this sort."

"We had a bit of luck there," said Manifold. "If you look at the back, you'll see that it happened to be the last page in the book. So it's got the printers' mark on it. It's a tiny monogram. The letters are H and L. Scotland Yard have got very good indexes of things like that. Laundry marks, pawnbrokers' marks, printers' monograms. They identified it without any difficulty. Hobson and Langdale, of Chichester. We had Mr. Hobson out of bed before seven o'clock. It being a Sunday, he wasn't best pleased, but he confirmed it for us at once."

Mr. Fairfax said, "Yes, I see." He was recovering a little of his composure. "You realize that we have been using these little booklets ever since I came here, fifteen years ago."

"But these particular books haven't been used for fifteen years. Originally the firm was just Mr. Hobson and the mark was a capital letter H. When he took in Langdale last year, they changed the mark to the present one. Mr. Hobson looked up his records for us. The first lot of books they printed for you with the new mark on it was in January of this year."

Mr. Fairfax said, in the stifled voice of one who was being pressed against the wall by the weight of logic, "Anyone—I suppose—might have got hold of one of these."

"How do you suggest they would do that?"

"Well—found it lying about."

"It's possible, but hardly likely, don't you think? The slip hasn't been filled in with a boy's name, or signed. That makes it likely it was still *in* the book when it was torn out and used to wedge the window glass."

"Anyone might have got hold of a complete book, I suppose."

"I wanted to ask you about that. During term time all the masters carry one about with them. What do they do with them at the end of term?"

"They hand them in to me."

"And what do you do with them?"

Mr. Fairfax opened one of the drawers of his desk. He said, "I keep them in here. The one I've got here was Mr. Mollison's. I remember putting it away when he left at half term."

"You don't lock the drawer."

"Certainly not. Why should I?"

"Well, I suppose someone might have got hold of one. But this particular slip wasn't out of Mr. Mollison's book. Look. The last one, with the printers' mark on it, is still there." He was examining the book as he spoke. "Only six slips have been torn out. Might this be Mr. Mollison's *second* book? Might he have used one up entirely?"

"It's most improbable. He very rarely punished any boy in any way at all. I doubt if he issued three demerits in a term."

"I see. Well, it cuts down the possibilities, doesn't it?"

Mr. Fairfax, who had been watching the possibilities cut down in front of his own horrified eyes, said, "There *must* be some other explanation. What about the printers? They'd have spare copies."

"We've checked their records. They all seem to be in order. So many books printed, so many issued, so many in stock. And anyway, aren't you supposing something extraordinarily unlikely? That they kept back a whole book. Why? And that some-

139

one tore out the last page in it, the only one with their mark on it, and left it at the scene of the crime. Again, why?"

Mr. Fairfax said, "I'm looking for explanations because the only alternative seems to me to be totally unbelievable. That one of my staff here tortured and murdered a boy."

"Three boys," said Manifold.

There was a long silence.

Mr. Fairfax said, at last, "And it was to investigate this—this possibility that you came here?"

"Colonel Brabazon was able to arrange it."

"What I don't understand is why you didn't take me into your confidence at once."

"We couldn't."

"I fail to see why not."

"Until we had made one or two inquiries we couldn't be sure that it wasn't you we were after."

Mr. Fairfax's face had gone dark red. It was more than a blush. It was a rush of blood to the head, an engorgement caused by uncontrollable emotion or shock. He seemed to be fighting for breath.

Manifold said, speaking in the same level tones, "Of course, I was very pleased indeed when I found out that you couldn't possibly have had anything to do with it. I was pretty sure of that as soon as I had met you and talked to you, but it's a policeman's unhappy duty to suspect everyone."

"How—" croaked Mr. Fairfax. He was loosening his collar as though to let out the words that were choked in his throat.

"Lister was picked up between six and seven and was dead by a quarter past ten, thirty-five miles away from here. Unless you had suborned the entire fumigation department of the Chichester Borough Council, it was quite clear that you, and they, were working here until well after nine o'clock that night. Incidentally, they told me that your gardener and his boy were giving a hand. So that was two more out of the way."

"And Sergeant Baker."

"And Sergeant Baker, of course."

Mr. Fairfax seemed to be breathing more easily now. He said, "I take it that you didn't overlook the possibility that Mollison . . ."

"We didn't forget Mr. Mollison. He left here on the Thursday and went straight up to a youth hostel in the Lake District. The local police made some inquiries with the hostelkeeper. Mr. Mollison has been leading an exemplary life. He goes for long walks by day, including a little simple climbing and botanizing, comes home for a late tea, and is in bed every night by ten. Incidentally, the routine seems to be doing him good. In conversation with the hostelkeeper he has more than once expressed the view that he had made a serious mistake in running away from his job here. You might do worse than get in touch with him. I can give you his address."

"I might do that," said Mr. Fairfax. But he spoke absently. He wasn't thinking about Mr. Mollison. His mind was moving uneasily round the circumference of the narrowing circle. He said, "And is anyone else, as you put it, in the clear?"

Manifold said, "The only one with any sort of alibi is Warr. He says he went straight down to Mr. Merriam's house in the village and spent the rest of the day doing a number of household jobs. So far as the afternoon is concerned, several people saw him up a ladder mending the gutter. And Mr. Bishop, who lives next door, saw him mowing the lawn soon after tea. The later jobs were all indoors and for those we have only Miss Shaw—who could hardly be described as an independent witness. And Mr. Merriam himself, who could quite easily have been fooled, since he can't leave his chair."

"What about the others?"

"None of the others has any sort of alibi at all."

"But—they all gave accounts of themselves. . . ."

"They gave accounts of themselves," agreed Manifold. "In one case the account is unconfirmed. In a second case it was deliberately misleading. In the third case it was a lie. To take Latrobe

141

first. He told me he drove to Guildford and parked his car in one of the large free car parks near the theater. Then apparently he went round to two or three hotels and asked for a room. He can't remember which hotels he went to, and since it was Saturday night, and the first night of a very popular production at the Yvonne Arnaud Theater, Guildford was full of young people who had been improvident enough not to book rooms and were trying to do so at the last moment. We've made inquiries at the likely hotels. One of them thinks they remember a young man who might have been Latrobe asking for a room. None of the others remember him at all. After that he went back to the theater, was lucky enough to pick up a ticket, one that had been returned, had a bite to eat in the theater restaurant, watched the play, walked back after it to his car, and settled down to spend the night in it. He says he thinks there were other people doing the same thing, but he didn't make any contact with them. As soon as it was light he drove to his parents' home at Banstead and had breakfast. After that he's accounted for for the rest of the weekend."

"I don't see anything suspicious in that," said Mr. Fairfax.

"I didn't say that it was suspicious. I said that it was unconfirmed."

"In any event I should have thought that he was the last person in the world to hurt a boy."

"He takes a somewhat romantic view of them," said Manifold dryly. "On the whole, I should have been inclined to agree with you, but for one point, which I'll come to in a moment. Let me deal with the other two first. Mr. Diplock, when I asked him how he had spent the weekend, said that he had stayed with his aunts in London. That is true. What he did not make clear, and it has taken a good deal of tactful inquiry to elicit it, is that he did not arrive home until two o'clock on Sunday morning. One of the neighbors says that she was woken up by his arrival in a taxi and the argument about the fare which followed."

"Has he offered any explanation?"

"He hasn't been asked for an explanation yet."

An expression that flashed across Mr. Fairfax's mind at this moment was one that he had often read in the papers: "Assisting the police in their inquiries." He saw Mr. Diplock, seated upright on a hard chair, fencing pedantically with the questions put to him by an irate inspector.

He said, "You mentioned a deliberately untrue statement."

"That was the Commander. I'm afraid his account of what he did that weekend was totally inaccurate. Inquiries have been made at the pub in the village where he says he spent Saturday night. In fact, that particular place stopped taking in residents almost a year ago. There are a couple of cottages in the village which offer bed and breakfast, but neither of them had a visitor that weekend."

"Why on earth should he lie about a matter like that?"

"He's an odd character," said Manifold. "Did you know that he was a night walker?"

"A night walker?"

"On two or three nights in the week he leaves this place around eleven o'clock and goes for a walk across the common."

"He's very keen on regular physical exercise."

"Certainly. But it seemed to be an odd time of night to take it. I discovered it by accident. I had periodical reports to make to Colonel Brabazon and the easiest way of keeping in touch was to walk to his house on the other side of the common. On several occasions I nearly bumped into the Commander. On one occasion I did bump into him, rather hard. I had been asked to check the cars in the staff garage—with particular reference to their tires. The Commander caught me at it when he was coming back from one of his rambles."

"What did he say?"

"He didn't have time to say anything."

"Didn't he recognize you?"

"Apparently not. It was dark inside the shed, and I took him by surprise. He hit his head on one of the cars as he went down, and was dazed for a bit. I waited up for him, in case he was worse than I imagined, but he didn't need medical attention. He's got quite a thick skull."

"But why didn't he report it? Why didn't he say something next morning?"

"That," said Manifold, "was one of the most intriguing aspects of the whole affair. It seemed to indicate that he wasn't anxious for inquiries to be made about his nocturnal expeditions."

"If it has to be one of them," said Mr. Fairfax, his lips contracting into a spasm of distaste, "it sounds as though Commander Gaze would be your most likely candidate. And yet I find it impossible to believe."

"Impossible?"

"I've known them all for a number of years. Seen them at work. Seen them with the boys." Anger was ousting shock. "Really, you've put me in an intolerable position. If I am to believe what you have told me, how can I go on working with them, entrusting my boys to them?"

"What's the alternative?"

"To get rid of them all, and start again with an entirely new staff."

"Wouldn't that be unfair to three men out of four?"

"You talk like that because you're a policeman, not a schoolmaster." A sense of outrage was thickening his voice. "I read in the paper what the man did to that boy. He tortured him before he killed him. How can I look at a man, and think of him doing it, without being sick?"

Manifold said, very patiently, "There's only about two weeks of this term left. I can promise you this: We'll have caught him before the end of term."

"How can you be sure?"

"He's between two fires. The internal investigation that I've been put here to conduct. And a much larger, slower, more certain investigation that's closing in on him from outside. If he hadn't been a man of very steady nerve, I think he'd have done something stupid already. It can't be long now."

Mr. Fairfax gave a short, bitter laugh. He said, "One of the most difficult things is going to be to remember to go on treating you as a schoolmaster."

"You've been doing all right so far," said Manifold. He was relieved to note that the first shock had expended itself. "Keep it up. Talking of which, I believe I'm meant to be taking prep. I'd better be off."

There was something else. It was at the back of Mr. Fairfax's mind. Manifold had reached the door before he remembered it. He said, "When you were talking about Latrobe, you said that there was one thing which might have made you suspect him."

"There's a theory," said Manifold, "but it's no more than a theory at the moment, that the man might have induced boys to accept a lift by dressing up as a woman."

The architect who had originally converted Trenchard House into a school had constructed a study for the headmaster at the back of the entrance hall, up a flight of six steps, at entresol level. He had so arranged it that this room led, in turn, up a further short flight, to a corridor in the private part of the house. This was very convenient since it enabled the headmaster to make public appearances from his study, but to disappear, at will, into his own quarters. It had another result, which Lucy Fairfax had discovered by accident. She had found that if she sat on the edge of the bed in their bedroom, which was beside the study and slightly above it, she could hear, by some trick of acoustics, everything that was said in the study. This had been a source of considerable entertainment. She had listened to parents being blarneyed, masters being rebuked, boys being punished. But she had never before listened to anything half as interesting as the conversation she had just managed to overhear.

Manifold's last remark seemed to cause her such intense amusement that she relaxed onto the bed and positively shook with laughter.

16

"I promised Fairfax that we'd nail him by the end of term," said Manifold. "And it ought to have been easy enough. I thought I could do the job in a few days. I mean, living right among them. Actually, I'm as far from it now as I was when I first started. The trouble is, I'm beginning to believe that this end of it isn't really a police job at all. It's a job for a professional psychiatrist."

"My dear chap," said Colonel Brabazon. "In that case, why not consult one?"

"Consult a psychiatrist?"

"Why not? If this was a case involving computers you'd go to a computer expert, wouldn't you? Or if it were old coins you'd consult a—I never can remember that word."

"A numismatist."

"Right. A numismatist."

"Had you anyone particular in mind?"

"Certainly. Go straight up to London and have a word with Dr. Sampson. I'll warn him to expect you. And we'll send him copies of all the technical reports. It'd be better if he could see these people himself, but that might be difficult in the circumstances. However, you can let him have the details of their past lives, and so on. And give him your own impressions of them. And don't forget to take him copies of those remarkably good photographs you were showing me. How did you get Mr. Diplock to hand them over?"

"I told him I had connections with a photographic publisher who would be very interested to see them."

"Did he believe you?"

"It's difficult to know what Mr. Diplock believes."

The general police view of psychiatrists is that they are people who tell lies in court to gain acquittals for people the police have sweated blood to put there. They were prepared to make a cautious exception in the case of Dr. Sampson for various reasons, some of which were not, perhaps, entirely logical.

George Earle Sampson was a qualified doctor who had specialized in three different fields. He had started his professional career as a pathologist, and had moved on from there to the field of nervous diseases. Having thus studied, as he pointed out, the effects of violence and shock on the human body and on the human nerves, it had been a logical progression to move on and consider the effect of like forces on the human mind.

He very rarely appeared in court and when he did, spoke the truth as he saw it. In appearance he resembled a bull walrus, and he had played water polo for England.

He said, "You realize that what Brabazon really expects me to do is to go off into a trance and pick the man for you by divination."

"He's got great confidence in you," said Manifold tactfully.

"And you know why? It's because once when I was staying with him, I told him that the young man who'd come down to audit his farm accounts was a crook. I didn't do *that* by psychiatry. I happened to notice he was wearing hand-lasted shoes and an Ibol wrist watch. You can't do that on a junior accountant's pay. These are very good photographs. Is this the photographer?"

"That's Mr. Diplock. It's one he must have taken of himself. He's got one of those remote-control gadgets. He takes a lot of pictures without people knowing he's doing it."

"Just so. And of course this is the only one which is no use to us."

"Why?"

"Well, since it's a picture of himself," said Dr. Sampson reasonably, "he must surely have known he was taking it. Unless he did it in his sleep. That means that what we've got here is his public face. In the other cases, since I assume they had no idea they were being photographed, we've got their private faces. Very private, in some cases." He was staring, fascinated, at the reflection of Lucy Fairfax, caught in the glass. "Introduce me to these people. Who's this thin young man?"

"Constance Latrobe, aged twenty-four. French father, English mother. Educated at the lycée in Kensington and at London University. Good second in the English School. Keen on acting and directing and a flair for both. When he was at London he put on and acted in a modern-dress production of *The Taming of the Shrew* which got considerable acclaim from professional critics."

"What part did he take?"

"He played Katherina."

Dr. Sampson grunted. "And being only twenty-four, do I take it this is his first job?"

"Correct. He's been at Trenchard House for three years."

"Anything you noticed about him particularly?"

"Well, he's in love with one of the boys. Ben Sacher's son, Jared."

"Photograph?"

"In this group. He's the one in the middle."

"Good-looking boy. How old?"

"Nearly fourteen. Mental age sixteen plus."

"They grow up quicker than we do," said Dr. Sampson. "When you say Latrobe's in love with him . . ."

"I meant precisely that. Sacher is the object of his affections. At a respectful distance. I'm quite sure he's never even touched him."

"How do you know that?"

"Because the other boys, including Sacher, pull his leg about it unmercifully. If he had, they wouldn't."

"You can leave the psychology to me," said Dr. Sampson. He considered the photograph. Latrobe had been caught in the full light of day, half closing his eyes as he stared into the sun, which threw into relief the high cheekbones and the hollows under them. The mouth was open in a smile which showed very regular teeth and the tip of his tongue peeping between them.

Dr. Sampson picked up the next photograph.

"And this young man?"

"Nigel Warr. Chelborough and Cambridge. Natural athlete. Rugby football, cricket, tennis, squash. You name it, he plays it and plays it well. Totally unintellectual. Totally unambitious. Engaged to the assistant matron."

"Photograph of her?"

"This one."

"Well, well," said Dr. Sampson, after an appreciative pause. "He's got good taste. I'd guess that's what female novelists refer to delicately as a body made for love."

The photograph had been taken in the school swimming pool, which the staff were allowed to use in the early evening, when the boys were doing prep. Elizabeth was standing on the end of the springboard, with her hands raised, ready to dive.

"And who's the other female?"

"That's our Lucy. Mrs. Fairfax."

The joint photograph was one of Mr. Diplock's cattier efforts. The contrast between the two women, seen side by side, in bathing suits, was striking. Lucy was sitting on the side of the bath, one foot dangling in the water, the other foot on the edge, with the leg bent. The way she was sitting emphasized the heaviness of her body, the overfull breasts, beginning to sag, the strong, almost masculine muscles in the arms and legs.

Dr. Sampson said, "It wouldn't call for very acute psychological insight to suggest that perhaps the two ladies don't get on very well together."

"They loathe each other's guts."

"Please try to be a little more precise."

Manifold said, "Sorry. That *was* rather a loose expression." He paused to collect his thoughts. "When Lucy talked to me about Elizabeth she didn't exactly run her down, not in so many words. The line she took was that Elizabeth was a girl of remarkably forceful character, who's hooked a weak-minded male creature and will marry him mainly for the fun they'll have in bed."

"Most of them don't wait to get married nowadays."

Manifold thought about this. He said, "She's not promiscuous. I should put it rather that she realizes that providence has given her a lot of bargaining power with that body of hers and she's prepared to use it shrewdly to achieve her own ends."

"Can't blame her for that. Now let's hear Elizabeth on Lucy."

"The line she takes is that she pities her, condemned to live all her life in a place that's intellectually beneath her, married to an unsatisfactory husband."

"Is he impotent?"

"I did wonder. They've got no children and would clearly like them."

"Is that him?"

"Those are all Mr. Fairfax, yes."

Mr. Diplock had produced for him three photographs of the headmaster. In the first of them he was talking to Colonel Brabazon. In the second, to a young man in rimless glasses whom he had identified as the absent Mr. Mollison. In the third, to a very small and frightened-looking boy. Dr. Sampson spread them, side by side, on his desk and stared down at them, his walrus mustache twitching with amusement.

He said, "The three faces of authority. You're right, the man's a genius. That chap Diplock, I mean. He's wasted as a schoolmaster. He ought to be running a photographic studio. Tell me more about Mr. Fairfax."

"I didn't bring the detailed report on him, because he's out of the hunt. He's got an absolutely watertight alibi."

"Don't talk to me about alibis," said Dr. Sampson sharply. "I'm not a policeman. I'm a scientist. I want *all* the facts, not just a selection that you happen to consider important."

"I'll tell you what I can remember. His father was a First World War hero. D.S.O. and bar and a lot of other gongs, but a good head on him, too. Stayed on in the army, was a brigadier in the early thirties and had a command in Palestine. He might have gone right to the top—after all, Monty was a brigadier in Palestine at that time—but he was very badly injured when his car was blown up by terrorists. He was invalided out, went into the City and made a lot of money. He had had two daughters in the early twenties and our chap, Thomas Edward, was born in 1927. He seems to have been terrified of his father, who was a real old-fashioned domestic tyrant. He left Wellington in 1945, having missed a place at university, and took up prep school mastering, I should guess, in order to get away from home. Five years later his father killed himself, his wife and one of his daughters in a car smash. That left Thomas with enough money to buy in at Trenchard House. He bought his senior partner out ten years ago and has been running it ever since."

"How did you get all this stuff?"

"In this particular case? I gather one of our fatherly superintendents went and chatted up the surviving sister."

Dr. Sampson was examining the three photographs with minute care. He said, "An early history like that could very well be a contributory cause of impotence. He might get over it if he'd submit to shock treatment."

"He's had a few shocks already this term," said Manifold. "That's Mr. Diplock. A professional prep school master. Three schools before Trenchard House. First one in Farnham. Second one up in Scotland at Kirkmichael, near Inverness. That was really a composite school, all ages from eight to eighteen. I gather he didn't like it much. Came south again to a school at Broadstairs. After that Trenchard House. The details are all in that dossier. The scholastic agents turned them up for us. He's a bachelor, lives with two aged aunts. Indulges in mild foreign travel in the summer holidays. Hobbies: Lepidoptera, philately, numismatics and photography, in that order."

"What does he do in the winter—hibernate?"

"He does look a bit like a tortoise. He's quite a shrewd old boy, really."

"Why do you say old? He doesn't look much more than fifty."

"Come to think of it, that's right," said Manifold. "He strikes you as old because he's cultivated an old man's habits. It's a Mr. Chips syndrome. The pottering and peering and the wisecracks fired off in a creaking voice. The boys imitate him beautifully."

"He's probably imitating himself most of the time," said Dr. Sampson. "Who's this?"

"Gregory Gaze. Lieutenant Commander R.N., retired. Prewar Dartmouth cadet. Class of 1938. Sublieutenant 1940. Lieutenant 1942. War service mainly in the Far East. Sound, but not outstanding. No merits, no demerits. Made lieutenant commander in 1952. Left the navy in 1968."

"Still a lieutenant commander?"

"Yes."

"Passed over for promotion. Could be the basis of an inferiority complex. Do the boys like him?"

"Well enough. He gives them the old sea-dog line. The younger ones swallow it. Early morning runs for health, late night walks for sex."

"Sex?"

"He's having it off with a woman who runs a riding stable on Tinmans Common. I didn't tell the head about it because I didn't really think it was fair. It's a huge, rambling old place. Pretty soon we're going to have to search it."

"Why?"

"Easy place to hide a car."

Dr. Sampson wasn't interested in cars. He was sizing up the face. He said, "Naval officers are deceptive people. They're usually type-cast as bluff, simple extroverts. Probably on account of their bluff, simple faces. Actually, their training, and the lives they have to lead, are calculated to produce the most complex introverts. Haven't you got any more? There must be some other men round the place."

"Mr. Bishop, who comes in twice a week to teach carpentry. Charlie Happold, the gardener, and young Richard, who helps him."

"Then why have you left them out? Any of them could have picked up one of those bits of paper you seem to set such store by."

"I suppose it's no use pointing out that Mr. Happold is nearly seventy and young Richard not yet seventeen. And that both of them were busy, at the time that matters, helping Mr. Fairfax to disinfest classrooms."

"Never leave a job half done. I should have thought your training would have taught you that. What about Mr. Bishop?"

"I understand that he's lived all his life in the village, and that his father and grandfather were carpenters before him. His great-great-grandfather probably helped to build Trenchard House."

Dr. Sampson was searching among the mass of papers on his desk. He said, "There's one report here. It's the final report from Central Research at Aldermaston. I don't know if you've read it or, if you *have* read it, whether you understood what they were getting at. What they're saying is that there is no evidence, from the boy's clothing or body, that any sexual act took place at all."

Manifold stared at him. "I thought all sadists . . ."

"There's no such thing as a typical sadist. Get that idea out of your head. Sadism's a natural instinct. All young children are sadists."

"All boys, you mean."

"*All* children. I have two angelic little daughters. At least that's the way I thought about them until I found them one day. They'd tied up another little girl and were having great fun stinging her with nettles. No. It's something we're lumbered with. It could all be part of nature's plan to keep the human race going, because as soon as we reach puberty, in most cases sadism gets sublimated into sex."

"But not in all cases?"

"In a few cases it gets mixed up with baser instincts. The power complex, for instance. When a tycoon sacks a couple of secretaries just to make the rest of the staff crawl, he's only a grown-up little boy pulling the wings off flies. Or it can get muddled up with patriotism. The Japanese prison guards and Gestapo torturers, our own commandos cutting sentries' throats. They all did it for their country. And look what happens when sadism gets sublimated by religion. That's what bred the Inquisition and the black-cowled monks chanting the Te Deum while they watched the victims of the auto-da-fé screaming at the stake."

Dr. Sampson was silent for a moment. Then he said, "But I'm not sure, on balance, that the most dangerous of the lot isn't what Kunzler, with a singularly unfortunate choice of words, calls the 'pure sadist.' He devotes a whole chapter to them in his book *The Causes of Perversion*. You ought to read it sometime."

"Why do you say 'most dangerous'?"

"Because for ninety-nine percent of the time, the pure sadist acts perfectly normally. It's only on the hundredth occasion that they feel this itch. They feel it more strongly than any sex or drink or drug addict. It's an itch which has to be satisfied, by performing an act of cruelty, or watching someone else perform one. There are clubs in Soho which cater to them."

Manifold said, "And there's no way of telling . . ."

"By their appearance? The ones I've met have looked as normal as you and me. There was a clergyman in our village when I was young. He preached the gospel of forgiveness every Sunday and disciplined his rather timid wife with a dog whip. I'm happy to remember that when the villagers found out they broke all his windows and used his whip on him. Some years ago I remember I had to give evidence in the case of a motherly old body who took in foster children. Her amusement was branding her small charges with red-hot wire. When the police found out about it and asked why none of them had complained, they said she had warned them that if they told tales she would cut their tongues out with her scissors."

Manifold repressed a shudder and said, "How does anyone ever know, until it's too late?"

"You have to spot the little red devil when he peeps out just for a split second. It isn't easy. But there's one thing you can be fairly certain about. In their rational moments they'll be feeling guilty about their addiction. Give you an example. Suppose you were a compulsive shoplifter. You know it's wrong and you know it's stupid, but when you see the stuff lying there your hand goes out and you pop it into your pocket. There are people like that. They're not professional thieves. Very often they are quite well off and in all other respects honest people. Now, if they happened to be present when a conversation turned to shoplifting, they'd be almost certain to give themselves away. Either they'd fight shy of the topic, or they'd talk a lot too much. They couldn't behave naturally. The red devil wouldn't let them."

"Interesting you should say that," said Manifold. "I do remember one discussion we had about corporal punishment. It was when Warr beat one of the boys for being impertinent to Elizabeth."

"Tell me about that."

When Manifold had told him, Dr. Sampson said, "I'd like you to remember every word of that conversation."

"I can't do that. But I can give you the gist of it. The Commander gave us the traditional guff. In his day, I gather, sublieutenants used regularly to beat snotties. Did 'em no harm. Turned them into damned good naval officers. Latrobe then blew his top. He took the line that while it might not harm the victim, it could turn the beater into a sadist."

"Did he actually use the word 'sadist'?"

"No. I don't think so. The Commander then accused him of being a trick cyclist."

"And the others?"

"Warr didn't say much. I think he made some crack about students. And Diplock turned the whole thing into a joke. I forget exactly how. I think it was about the staff biscuits."

"And that's all you can remember?"

"It was only a casual conversation."

"On a job like that you ought to carry a tape recorder," said Dr. Sampson sourly. "Well, there's plenty to do. You'll be pursuing the obvious lines, I take it."

"What particular lines," said Manifold cautiously, "did you have in mind?"

"For God's sake, you don't expect me to teach you police work, do you? *The obvious lines.* Get hold of someone who was a midshipman when Gaze was a sublieutenant. Find one or two boys who had just arrived at Chelborough when Warr was head of his house."

"How do we know he was head of his house?"

"If he was as good as that at games, he must have been. Get their opinion of him. Have inquiries made at Farnham, Kirkmichael and Broadstairs to see if there were any suspicious incidents in or near those places when Diplock was teaching there. And I don't only mean boys. Sadists often practice their abominations on animals. Cattle slashing, horse maiming, cutting up dogs and cats. And last but not least, give those photographs to the top vice-squad man at the Yard. I think it's Chief Inspector Taylor. He's their expert on Soho. Get him round the clubs which cater to sadism."

Manifold, who had been scribbling hard, said, "Anything else?"

"Yes," said Dr. Sampson seriously. "Get a move on. He's got to be stopped before he does it again."

17

It was far from clear how the news had leaked out. Jared Sacher had said nothing. And yet by the Friday of that week every boy in the school, from McMurtrie at the top to Holbrow Three, who was really too young to be at school at all and was only there because his two brothers were there already, knew for a fact that Manifold was a policeman.

This was the cumulative result of a number of impressions rather than any actual leakage of information. It started with a report, disbelieved at first, that on the night of the attempted kidnapping Mr. Manifold and Sergeant Baker had been observed, from an upper dormitory window, coming back together from the direction of the main gate. They were said to have been coming back furtively. The reporter of this was the Pakistani boy, Palel Major, who had been responsible for the visit of the fumigation department at half term. He was not popular, and anything he said was discounted.

In spite of this, the rumor grew in strength. Boys in a closed community become very sensitive to the nuances of personal relationships. They had already noted the way in which Manifold spoke to his colleagues and to the headmaster. They now took note of the way the headmaster spoke to him.

The rumor hardened steadily, and by the end of the week had become accepted truth which no denial would shake.

In practice it made very little difference. It was assumed that he was there to watch over Jared Sacher, and would remain on guard for the rest of the term. They had previously accepted the fact that he could not be fooled with. The news of the summary way in which he had dealt with One-B had dispelled any doubts on this score. The fact that he was now armed also with the panoply of the law only added a touch of glamour to a reputation that was already established.

If Manifold was aware of this change of status he gave no sign of it, and no boy was bold enough to question him. He did, however, have two unexpected conversations, both of them on the Friday following the cricket match.

The first occurred as he was coming back from the village after lunch. Halfway down the drive, set back among the shrubs on the left-hand side, was a small octagonal building. It was the same age as the house and was built of the same brick. The boys, who made up stories about everything, had decided that it was a sentry box, placed there by the nabob to guard himself against the enemies from India who would be after his blood.

The voice of Lucy Fairfax hailed him from the dark interior. "Stick 'em up, copper. You're covered."

Manifold swung off the drive, crossed the rough grass and stood in the doorway. Lucy was sitting on one of the stone seats that ran round the inside of the building. She had been absent from lunch, and Manifold realized that she had had rather more than her customary two glasses of pre-lunch sherry.

"Take the weight off your feet," she said. "Why are policemen supposed to have large feet? You've got rather nice feet."

Manifold came in and sat down beside her. His bulk had been blocking the narrow doorway. When he moved he let in a shaft of sunlight and he was able to see her face. The expression on it disturbed him.

"You remember that little talk we had," she said. "Soon after you came. I told you you weren't a schoolmaster, didn't I? And I was right, wasn't I?"

She put one hand on his arm, but Manifold had the impression that it was more a move to anchor him to her side than a gesture of affection.

He said, "It seems to be fairly common knowledge now that I'm here to help Sergeant Baker look after Jared."

"It may be common knowledge, Ken. But I'm not one of the common people. Inspector? Chief Inspector? Superintendent?"

"Detective Chief Inspector is the correct title. But Ken will do for the moment."

"All right, Ken. I'll confess to you. I know exactly why you're here. You're looking for a man. A man who assaults little boys. And, Ken, I can help you catch him. Because I can tell you something. Something you'd never guess, not if you tried for a hundred years." The grip tightened until he could feel her long fingers digging into the muscles of his arm.

He said, "All right, I'll buy it."

"It isn't a him, Ken. It's a her."

"You're talking about Elizabeth, I suppose."

"Of course. When I heard about the man being supposed to dress up as a woman, I couldn't help laughing. Think of old Dip in a wig and falsies. He'd look like a pantomime dame."

She realized that she had lost her audience. Manifold had jerked free of her and was standing up. He said, savagely, "I suppose your husband couldn't keep his mouth shut. How many more people have you talked to about this?"

"It wasn't my husband who told me. He never tells me anything. And I haven't said anything to anyone."

"If he didn't tell you, who did?"

"I heard it. From our bedroom. I can hear everything that's said and done in that study."

Manifold said, "I see." Something of the coldness in his voice got through to Lucy's alcohol-inflated mind. She said, "I promise you, Ken, I haven't said a word."

"When you heard me talking to your husband about this, I gather you thought it was funny."

"Not funny, really. Just the thought of someone dressing up as

159

a woman. When it really was a woman all along."

"Have you got any reason to suppose it was Elizabeth?"

"But of course I have. Can't you see, Ken? She's just the sort of person who would. She was a nurse. You knew that."

"Yes."

"In a mental hospital. You know the sort of things that go on there. You read about them in the papers."

"Go on."

"And she's strong. Much stronger than you'd think. Nurses in those places are trained in dealing with patients. She'd have no difficulty with a boy."

"And that's the whole of your reason for making this accusation."

"No. That isn't all. It's difficult to explain, Ken. But she's hard. Perhaps it's easier for a woman to see than a man. It's an inner hardness. It doesn't give itself away, but you can feel that it's there, all the time."

Her voice died away into silence. Lucy gave a sudden shudder. She said, "It's cold in here. I don't know why I came. I'm going back."

Manifold was blocking the doorway again. He made no move to let her past. He said, "Since you know so much, I'm going to tell you a little more. And I'm going to give you a warning. It's *not* a woman who has been doing these things. It's definitely a man. He's been seen, by at least four people. Not close enough, or for long enough, to be recognized. But no question that he's a man. And he's on his own. If there had been a second person at the scene of the crime, the signs would have been picked up. That information is confidential. You understand me."

Lucy said, in a very small voice, "Yes."

"We're dealing with a man who has got to be caught. The net's closing in on him. It may be a matter of days. It may be only hours. But if he was warned, if he knew what we were up to, he might still slip out or destroy the vital evidence. If I had any reason to suppose that you had repeated what you managed to overhear, or what I've just told you, I'd have you taken down to the police station and held there."

Lucy said, her face white, "You couldn't do that."

"I most certainly could. You'd be assisting the police with their inquiries."

"It'd be against the law."

"In this particular case," said Manifold calmly, "I don't give a bent nickel if I have to break every rule in the book. Do I make myself clear?"

"Yes," said Lucy faintly.

"That's the entrance to the duke's palace," said Mr. Bishop, "and though I shouldn't say it, I think it's rather smart."

"It's lovely," said McMurtrie.

"Very ducal," agreed Jared.

"Are you sure it won't blow over?" said Billy Warlock. "Father was doing Shakespeare in the open air once, and Macbeth's castle fell on his head. He had concussion for a week."

"If it's wet or windy, we'll be in here," said Mr. Bishop. "If we're outside, we'll fix it to the balustrade. It'll be all right."

"What are those other bits?"

"That's the back of the lady's house. You'll have a few bushes in tubs out in front, so you know you're in the garden. Then you move them away, and bring those two side bits forward—"

"Flats," said Roger Warlock firmly.

"Is that what you call them? Mr. Latrobe sketched them out for me."

That Mr. Bishop should have turned out to be a scenic artist as well as a carpenter was no surprise to them. They knew him to be a versatile man.

McMurtrie said, "I think they're stupendous." As he said this he caught Mr. Bishop's eye, and jerked his head very slightly to the right, moving away to the far end of the gym. When they were out of earshot he said, "I was going to ask your right reverence if you'd do something for me. Jared and Jos and I were planning to celebrate the last night of our stay in this abode of learning by having a little celebration."

"A dormitory feast, eh?"

"Something of the sort."

"Sausage rolls, doughnuts, ginger pop."

McMurtrie shuddered. He said, "You've been reading too many comics. That sort of thing went out with Billy Bunter. I meant a real celebration."

"And had you anything particular in mind?"

"Actually what we wanted was a few bottles of bitter lemon and half a bottle of vodka."

Mr. Bishop opened his mouth, and then shut it again. He said, "I could get it. But I'm not going to bring it up to the school. It's all very well for you. If you got caught, you'd just get walloped. If I got caught, I'd lose this job, and I've been doing it too long to want to do that."

"Of course I'll come and fetch it. We don't want you to take any risks at all. And if it's found, I'll say I brought it back when I went out with my father, after the cricket match."

"When do you want it by?"

"I'll come down on Monday, as soon as it gets dark. That's T.E.F.'s night for bridge with the vicar. It'll be quite safe the way I come. I'll be out and back again in twenty minutes. No trouble at all."

"I hope not," said Mr. Bishop. "I really do hope not."

"You can fool some of the people all the time," said Elizabeth, "and all the people some of the time, but you can't fool me."

"That wasn't what President Lincoln said."

"It's what I'm saying, and I mean it."

She was lying beside him stretched out along the edge of the swimming pool, one hand paddling in the water.

"All right," said Manifold sleepily. "I can't fool you." He had had a long, lazy swim and had dried off in the sun and was feeling more relaxed and happy. The fact that Elizabeth had come and laid herself down beside him increased his happiness. She really was a beauty. What had a dumb athlete like Warr, a piece of totally brainless cheesecake, done to deserve her?

"You're a policeman, aren't you?"

Manifold turned his head to look at her. It was the proportion of leg to body that took a girl out of the merely attractive class and made her seductive. Also something to do with the way the legs joined the body. Breasts were important, but irrelevant. It was the curve of the hips and the buttocks and that fascinating little hillock—

"Stop smacking your lips," said Elizabeth, "and listen to what I'm saying."

"I'm listening. I'm a policeman. Even Holbrow Three knows that. I'm told he's plucking up courage to ask me to sign his autograph book."

"But you didn't come here to keep an eye on Jared."

"Oh? Then what did I come here for?"

"I'm not quite sure. But I've got a theory about it."

"Tell me."

"You've been asking a lot of questions about what people were doing the weekend before you came. The twelfth and thirteenth of June. That can't have anything to do with Jared. He was up in London with his father."

"Policemen enjoy asking questions."

"So I came to the conclusion that it was something that happened that weekend. Some crime. A pretty serious crime if Scotland Yard—you are from Scotland Yard, aren't you?"

"I'm admitting nothing."

"Anyway, you're obviously quite a superior sort of policeman. A cut above Sergeant Baker."

"Sergeant Baker's a very good policeman indeed."

"He's a darling. But the point is that if someone like you was sent down, it must have been a serious crime. Something that people were really getting uptight about. And it must have happened somewhere in this part of the world. So I got hold of all

163

the papers that came out that Monday and there was only one that seemed at all probable. It was that kid Ted Lister."

As Elizabeth said this she turned her head to look at him. Manifold said, with what he hoped was the right degree of indifference, "Lister. The name certainly rings a bell."

"The boy was tortured and killed."

"Place near Farnham. Yes, I remember it. And it did happen that weekend."

"All right," said Elizabeth. "Be cagey about it. I suppose you have to be. I think the police found something to suggest that the killer might have come from here or hereabouts. Tell me I'm imagining things."

"You're imagining things."

Elizabeth gave a little shiver and said, "I hope so. It's not a very comfortable idea. I don't really much like thinking about it."

"Then why *are* you thinking about it?"

"When I realized that you were interested in what everyone was doing that weekend, naturally I started to think about it, too. I mean, I knew where Nigel and I were, and I thought I knew where T.E.F. and Lucy and Sergeant Baker and Charlie Happold and young Richard were. I thought they were all busy disinfesting."

"You *thought* they were?"

"That's right. We heard such a lot about all the work they'd done, sealing up windows and doors and moving furniture and working away like beavers until nine o'clock at night to get it finished, and it was only when I was talking to Charlie about it that I realized that he hadn't actually seen Lucy at all."

"Perhaps she was doing a separate job."

"Right. That was what I thought. So I had a word with Richard. And with the sergeant. He was all over the place. If she'd been there, he'd have been bound to see her."

"When did anyone remember seeing her last?"

"As far as I can gather, about teatime. I've no doubt T.E.F. would know where she was. But I hardly liked to raise the question with him."

"I expect there's some fairly simple explanation," said Manifold.

"Oh, I expect there is," said Elizabeth. She rolled over onto her other side. The movement brought her face close to his. He could look down into her guileless blue eyes.

The door in the wall behind them crashed open. Nigel bounded in. He was wearing only a pair of leopard-skin bathing trunks and was carrying a towel. He hurled the towel into the corner, shouted, "Tarzan love Jane," and cleared both the bodies on the edge of the pool, turning the jump at the last moment into a jackknife dive.

With a quick wriggle Elizabeth went after him. Manifold saw her following him as he swam under water. She was faster than he was, and managed to catch hold of his ankles. They surfaced at the far end of the pool in a splutter of foam.

"If you don't come clean," said McMurtrie, "not a single solitary drop of vodka will you get."

"Not even a drop of bitter lemon," said Joscelyne.

"I can't," said Jared.

They were sitting, cross-legged, on McMurtrie's bed. Outside another July day had died in red glory. There was a luminous quality about the dusk.

"Why can't you tell us?"

"Because I promised not to."

"Even if we swear on the Bible not to tell anyone else?"

"Well . . ." said Sacher.

McMurtrie sensed a weakening. He said, "When a soldier was taken prisoner by the Japs, my father told me, he was allowed to give them military information. That was to save him from being tortured. Suppose we were going to torture you. Then you'd be excused if you broke your word and told us."

"Perhaps. If I really thought you were going to."

"Oh, we'll torture you all right, won't we, Jos?"

"Rather," said Joscelyne.

"How?"

"What we'll do is, we'll tie your wrists to the head of your bed, and Jos will sit on your legs and I'll tickle your stomach. You're ticklish, aren't you?"

"Very."

"In a story I read," said Joscelyne, "an Indian rajah tickled one of his wives to death with a peacock feather. He went on until she had a fit. So you see—"

Jared said, "I can see I've got no choice."

McMurtrie and Joscelyne settled down happily. They knew that Jared was longing to tell them. He said, "Everything I said was lies. That is, from the moment we came in sight of the car. The two men each had hold of one of my arms. I couldn't see the driver at all. I think they had expected him to be outside the car waiting for them and they were worried because he wasn't there. The tall man, who was on my right, said something like, 'Where's Rex?' I think it was Rex. And he half let go of my arm. At that moment someone who had been standing behind the car, in the darkness under the tree, said, 'Down, Jared. Flat on your face.' Well, you remember what your father told us. I recognized Mr. Manifold's voice, and without giving it another thought I flopped down on the ground."

"Did they let go of you?"

"The tall man did. The other one clung on and came down onto his knees with me. Then there was this sound. Like a cork coming out of a bottle, only much louder, and with a sort of twang to it. The tall man spun round and came down beside me."

"Dead?" breathed McMurtrie.

"I don't know. I was too scared to notice much. I think the other man was as frightened as I was. I could feel him shaking. Then Mr. Manifold and Sergeant Baker came out from behind the car. They both had guns. They handcuffed the man who was holding me and bundled him into the back of the car. The driver was there already. I couldn't see if he was dead or just unconscious. Then the van arrived."

"What van?"

"It was a big furniture van. It must have been standing outside, on the road, because I heard it start up, and it backed through the gate. Some men jumped out and opened the door at the back, and they put down a sort of ramp, and Sergeant Baker drove the car up the ramp into the van, and the tall man was lifted into the back with it, and the van drove off. The whole thing was over in less than five minutes. It was after the van had gone that I heard the front door of the school opening and T.E.F. shouting something."

"He was yelling at the kids to get back to bed," said Joscelyne.

"What were you doing?" said McMurtrie.

"I was sitting down beside the path, shivering. When the van had gone, Mr. Manifold came back and sat down beside me. He said, 'Here's where you've got to do some playacting. Do you think you can?' My teeth were still chattering. I said, 'I'll d-d-d-do what I can.' "

The boys laughed.

Jared said, "When I'd got my wits back a bit, Mr. Manifold told me what to do, and what I'd got to say. 'Don't make it elaborate,' he said. 'You can think out the details later. For now, just say, "They let me go." If anyone starts asking questions, give them a dopey sort of stare. And if the going gets rough, you can always pass out.' So that's what I did."

"Goodness," breathed Joscelyne.

"Some people have all the luck," said McMurtrie.

"It wasn't funny at the time," said Jared. "Not a bit funny."

As he lay in bed, trying to get to sleep, McMurtrie acted through the whole episode, with himself taking the leading part. To stand, in the darkness, with a gun in one hand, to see Jared drop, and then to shoot, point-blank, at the tall man and watch him keel over. The thought of it sent a prickle of excitement which started in his stomach, went all the way down into his thighs and seemed to come out at the soles of his feet.

18

Detective Inspector Bob Taylor operated from West End Central Police Station and his manor included the square mile that is bounded by Oxford Street, Charing Cross Road, Shaftesbury Avenue and Wardour Street and is known as Soho.

He was a methodical man. He had recorded, in a filing system of computerized complexity, the names, assumed names, ages, personal descriptions, distinguishing characteristics, photographs and nearest known relatives of every prostitute, male and female, operating in his area. He charted their nesting habits and seasonal migrations with the accuracy and care of an ornithologist. He was particularly interested when they disappeared from their normal habitat. A surprising number of murder cases had originated from those filing cabinets.

He had, at that time, two regular assistants. Detective Sergeant Goodman, a stout, deliberate man approaching middle age, and Detective Sergeant Michael Appleyard, who was thinner and younger, though not quite as young as he looked.

Inspector Taylor displayed a handful of photographs to each of these assistants and explained the reason for the inquiry. He said, "You do the strippers, Goody. You can cover the kinky shops, Mike. I'll take the boss clubs. O.K.?"

Sergeant Goodman said, "Can we tell them what it's all about?"

"If you think it'll help."

"I think it would," said Sergeant Appleyard. "They don't like the idea of kids being messed about. We'll get more cooperation if we tell them."

"Tell them. But leave out names. And get a move on, both of you. I'm told it's urgent."

Sergeant Appleyard, who was as methodical as his chief, first compiled a list of the establishments he planned to visit, and then tackled them on a geographical basis, starting at the bottom of Frith Street and working north. The shops concerned sold a variety of goods, ranging from solid works like *The History of Flagellation and Torture* by a Reverend Gentleman to life-size inflatable female figures. ("Why be lonely at night? Clarissa is the perfect bedmate. Doesn't snore. Doesn't smoke in bed. Doesn't answer back. Available in three different colors.")

By four o'clock that afternoon, Sergeant Appleyard had told his story and shown his photographs to the proprietors of twenty-two shops. The results had been entirely negative. The owners, and their assistants, who were apt to take rather more careful note of the appearance of their customers than was usual in ordinary shops, were reasonably certain that they recognized none of the people concerned. Certainly none of them were regular customers. Appleyard returned to West End Central to take his weight off his feet and write his report.

While he wrote, he spread the photographs out once more on the desk in front of him. He knew, now, what had been worrying him all day. One of the photographs rang a very faint bell in his memory. The difficulty was that the routine of a policeman involves a good deal of looking at photographs and memorizing faces, and in the end one face is apt to become confused with another.

All that he was certain of was that it was some years ago, and was not connected with his present line of duty.

Sergeant Goodman, meanwhile, had been making a round of the strip clubs. Most of these were run by businessmen who spent their mornings in their offices worrying, like any other business-man, about rents, rates and rising prices and taxes. They knew Sergeant Goodman and received him, when they understood what he wanted, with sympathy.

"I guess you're barking up the wrong tree, Goody," said Rosy Rosenbaum. "A geezer like that wouldn't come here. He's not interested in the unveiled female form presented in fifty different artistic poses. He's just a plain sod, right?"

Sergeant Goodman agreed that that was right, but said that some people were ambidextrous.

"Could be," said Rosenbaum. "Have one of these cigars. Take one for your wife. I wouldn't think it very likely myself. Most of our regulars are highly respectable people. You know that one I was telling you about last time you was here. The one we call the Archdeacon. You know what he did last night? Came right up on the stage and started auctioning the girl's clothes. Talk about a laugh."

Sergeant Goodman said, "I didn't come here to listen to your filthy reminiscences, Rosy. Save 'em for your autobiography. All I want to know is, do you recognize any of these people?"

"I'd be lying if I said I did. Frank's got a good memory for faces. What do you say?"

Frank, who was the doorman and chucker-out, shook his head. One of them, he said, reminded him of a man he'd been in the army with. But come to think of it, he heard that he'd died.

It was at his eighth visit, at the Penny-Come-Quickly, a discreet and rather high-class club in Lord Scrope Street, that Sergeant Goodman struck pay dirt. The proprietor, a redheaded Irishman, known to all as Pat Murphy although his name, in fact, was Gavigan, paused at the fourth photograph and said, "Sure, now, that's a face I recognize. He's been here more than once."

"How long ago, Pat?"

"The last time would have been a month or so ago. I remember it well. We had a little trouble, which is not a thing I like with my regular clients at all."

"What sort of trouble?"

"He was trying to take photographs. We couldn't allow that. It embarrasses the girls."

"What happened?"

"There was what you might term a disputation. In the end we had to remove his camera. He was angry and used expressions which I'm sure he regretted afterwards."

"Have you got the camera?"

"Certainly not. We handed it back when he left. I'm telling you, we parted good friends."

"Can you fix the date?"

"It was a Saturday. I know that for sure."

Mr. Murphy consulted a calendar on the wall. It was illustrated, curiously enough, not with unclothed girls in provocative poses, but with three fluffy kittens with bows round their necks.

"It was the night we first showed our Hawaiian Speciality. You ought to see it, Sergeant. A treat for the whole family."

"I'll bring 'em along sometime. What day does that make it?"

"A month ago this Saturday that's coming. It would have been June twelfth."

"Ah, and you're sure it's this man?"

"Am I going to be called to swear to it in a court of law? You'll understand that I'm not anxious to give evidence against my own clients."

"If that man spent the evening here," said Sergeant Goodman, closing his notebook, "you're more likely to be giving evidence for him than against him."

Inspector Taylor paid only two visits, but they were to important people and in both cases he had to make an appointment by telephone. The first was to a chemist's shop in Barnaby Street. He introduced himself to the young man behind the counter, who disappeared through a door at the back of the shop. There followed a wait of nearly five minutes, during which the inspector sold a woman a bottle of hair dye and a man a box of throat

171

lozenges, stacking the money carefully on the counter. The young man then reappeared, and gestured to him to follow. The passage in which he found himself was so long that it was clear they were passing into the next house through an intervening opening. Finally they arrived at a white-painted door, decorated with handsome brass door fittings. The young man knocked, opened the door without waiting and motioned to the inspector to go in.

A small gray-haired lady was seated beside the window, which looked out onto a tiny scrap of garden. She said, "Sit down, Inspector Taylor. Or is it Chief Inspector now?"

"Not yet."

"It will be soon, I'm sure. What can I do for you?"

The inspector explained what he wanted and spread out the photographs on the end table beside her chair. She examined each of them with minute care, seeming to be more interested in the women than the men. She said, "Cruelty for the sake of cruelty. It's not a common disease. But a very unpleasant one when it does occur. It's not really in my line. You'll have to have a word with the Major."

"I'm seeing him this afternoon."

"I'll keep my eyes open, of course." She handed back the photographs, got to her feet and said, "No need to go back through the shop. I'll let you out by the front door."

As he walked down the sunlit street, the inspector reflected that you could never tell by appearances. Some of the stories he had heard about the half-dozen establishments which that little old lady ran, mainly for middle-aged gentlemen of odd tastes, had turned even his hardened stomach.

The second visit the inspector paid was to a firm of estate agents in a side turning off Soho Square. He was shown straight up to a room on the second floor, labeled "Managing Director." The man behind the desk did not get up, but waved the inspector to a chair. The inspector forgave him the discourtesy since he knew that the Major had lost the use of one leg as the result of a beating by Polish deserters soon after the war. His face was a map of the battles he had fought in his long, successful and unsavory life. The left side was seamed with lines and wrinkles. The right side was a pad of white and lifeless flesh, topped by a sightless eye, all that was left of the living face after an attack made on him by a woman with sulfuric acid.

The inspector spread his photographs on the desk. While he was talking, the Major kept his single good eye fixed on him and did not even look down at the photographs.

He said, "Is there a reward for this information?"

"Only the reward of helping to catch this man."

"If you're not offering a reward the matter can't be serious."

The inspector was too old a hand to show his annoyance. He said, smoothly, "We didn't think this was the sort of inquiry which would be helped by payments of money."

"I see." The Major shifted his gaze to the photographs, focusing his single spotlight on each in turn. Then he gathered them together and said, "I have never seen any of them. And I do not believe that any of them has been to any of my establishments. We examine our patrons very carefully before we admit them."

"I know you do. Well, thank you for trying."

The Major selected one of the photographs he was holding. He said, "If you had asked me, from my experience, which of these men was most likely to be the one you are looking for, I should have chosen him."

"That could be helpful," said the inspector. When he got out into the street, he took several deep lungfuls of what passes in Soho for fresh air.

Other policemen were active, too. Inquiries were being made in the area around Farnham. A doctor at Broadstairs who did a lot of work for the police was asked to turn up some of his old records. A sergeant of the Scottish constabulary who had spent most of his working life at Kirkmichael was recalled from his retirement at Kirriemuir and questioned closely.

Other people who were not, in the strictest sense of the word, policemen were working, too. Old school friends were meeting up, seemingly by accident, in the bars and smoking rooms of London clubs. The talk would turn, as such talk often does, to the heroes of the past. Nigel Warr? Bloody good stand-off half, said number one. Unlucky to have missed his blue. Wondered what had happened to him. You didn't see him playing for any of the top London clubs. Number two said he thought he had heard that he'd taken up schoolmastering. Number one thought this was a very good joke. When he fagged for Warr, he remembered one of his chores had been to do all his maths prep for him.

Old naval friends seemed to be encountering each other, too, and reliving, over a succession of pink gins, their early days in the Royal Navy.

A thin trickle of information from all these sources duly reached Superintendent Jock Anderson and Detective Inspector David Rew at their headquarters in the British Legion hut at Haydock Wood, a headquarters which, after four weeks, was beginning to wear the air of a permanent establishment.

There were four policemen permanently on duty in front of the bank of telephones and the walls were lined with large-scale and small-scale maps. One of the largest of the maps had been inset into a tabletop and was equipped with an electrical device by which, at the pressure of a selector in a row of switches, different lights in the map lit up and winked redly, like the eyes of tiny creatures caught in headlights at night.

As this information arrived it was sifted, pondered over and fitted into the picture that was slowly emerging.

On Sunday night three men sat late in Colonel Brabazon's study. They had been talking since ten o'clock and it was now nearly two.

The colonel seemed unaffected by the responsibilities of his position or the lateness of the hour. The noticeable changes, Manifold thought, were in Jock Anderson. He had the look of a man who had been working at full pitch for too long. The lines of strain were apparent on his thin face, but there was something else there, too. Was it the look of a general, at the crisis of a long and hard-fought battle, who suddenly sensed that the enemy was weakening and victory might be there for the taking? The pressure must be kept up for a little longer. Then he might relax and go to sleep.

Manifold hoped that he was wrong about this. It was a state of mind that he mistrusted. There might come a moment at which a single mistake could turn victory into disastrous failure, and a tired man might make that mistake.

"So that's the situation to date," said the colonel. "Mr. Diplock is definitely excluded. Not only have we had good reports from previous colleagues and found no single trace of previous outbreaks in any of the areas he's been associated with, but we are as certain as we can be, short of a formal identification parade, where he was from eight o'clock until midnight on the twelfth."

Manifold laughed. He said, "I hope, for his reputation, that we never have to demonstrate it in court. He once told me that the most fascinating part of his hobby was photographing animals in their natural surroundings. I thought he was referring to his aunts' goat, not the undraped beauties of the Penny-Come-Quickly."

"He was never very high on my list," said Anderson. "The man we're after is younger and stronger."

Manifold said, "I thought that one of the most curious results of the investigation in Soho was that a man they call the Major, who's an unquestioned expert in the byways of perversion, should have put a finger on Mr. Fairfax as the most likely candidate. I don't mean that he identified him. It was a spot selection made on the basis of the photographs alone."

"But he's definitely out of it," said the colonel. He sounded distressed.

"No question of that. Half a dozen people saw him and talked to him at the critical time. They're not so sure about Lucy Fairfax, though."

"I refuse to believe that the driver of that car was a woman," said Anderson. "Four witnesses said, without any qualification, that it was a man."

"I agree," said the colonel. "A man can dress up as a woman on the stage and get away with it. In real life you can always tell the difference, somehow. Incidentally, I gather we've eliminated Mr. Bishop, too."

"Yes. And he *was* a distinct possibility. I told you that the laboratory had identified fragments of hard wood on the blanket which the man was using. It was almost the only material clue we had, and it pointed to a carpenter or joiner. But unless six or seven of the Boxwood villagers are lying—and I see no reason why they should; they aren't all Bishop's friends by any means—it's certain that he was drinking in the bar of the Lion from seven to eight, and was back there from nine o'clock until closing time."

"I'm glad about that," said Colonel Brabazon. "I've always liked Stan Bishop. He did a lot of work for me on this house when I moved in. Have you got any more for us?"

"The rest of it is less definite. We've traced Mr. and Mrs. Fairfax back to the two schools they were at before they took over at Trenchard House. Both were well liked by the boys. He certainly wasn't a bully. Miss Shaw was a nurse at the Quaker Hospital at Caversham for two years. She only left because her stepfather had his stroke. The matron was very sorry to lose her. Warr gets a comparatively clean sheet from his contemporaries at Chelborough. Gaze isn't quite so good. Two senior naval officers independently described him as 'a bit of a brute.' And if you can say that about someone forty years after the event, he must have left a sting behind."

"It's not very conclusive."

"It doesn't prove anything," agreed Anderson. "It just adds a little to the picture. In my book there are just two people left. And if I'm right about either, I know where the car will be. If Gaze is our man, he must keep it at Huntsman's Castle. That's the place on the north edge of the common. I expect you know it, sir?"

"Yes," said Colonel Brabazon dryly. "And I know Mrs. Herbert, who runs the riding establishment there. Actually, she only uses part of it. It's a rambling old place, with fifty acres of paddock and woodland, and dozens of outhouses and sheds. You could hide half a dozen cars there. I take it the other man in your book is Latrobe? Where would he keep a second car?"

Anderson said to Manifold, "You mentioned in one of your reports that you had both the Warlock boys at the school."

"Roger and Billy? What about them?"

"You know their father's acting at Chichester this summer?"

"Yes. They told me. He's taken a house, a couple of miles out of town on the Bosham side."

"Lytham Hall," said Anderson. "That's a big place, too. Parts of it are said to be Roman. Lots of chances to hide a car. And I'm told that Latrobe's been down there a number of times."

"Likely enough," said Manifold. "Roger told me that Latrobe knew his father. Probably met him when he was acting up in London." He stopped to think about it, and then said, "It's plausible. Because I gather that their father is more or less camping out at Lytham Hall. His wife's keeping their other house going, and only comes down there for weekends. He sleeps in the house and someone comes in to cook his breakfast and clean up, but most of the time I should think the house and grounds are deserted. It was empty for more than a year before he took it."

The colonel said, "Another peg, gentlemen?"

When both men shook their heads, he got up, poured himself out a small one and stood with it in his hand. He said, "It's your show, Superintendent. But if I was in your shoes, I know what I'd do. I'd take twenty men and search both those places at first light tomorrow. If there's a car there, you'll find it."

"There's one thing that's stopping me doing just that," said Anderson. "Suppose it's a stolen car he's using. We know how careful he is. And one witness at least told us he was wearing gloves. Suppose he wore gloves all the time he was using the car. So no fingerprints. We find the car at one of these places, hidden in a shed some way from the house, perhaps. We can prove, without any difficulty, that it's the murder car. *But how do we prove it's got anything to do with our man?* And I mean prove it so that it'll stand up in a court of law."

Manifold and the colonel thought about this. The colonel said, "I see your point. What's your plan?"

"I'm going to have both those places watched, quietly. And I'm going to try to bolt our man. The first BBC announcement goes out tomorrow evening, on the six o'clock news. We're stepping it up, adding a little more detail each night. That way, I think we can break his nerve."

"And if you don't?"

"Then we shall have to try more direct action."

The colonel swallowed down his drink, looked at his watch and said to Manifold, "Can I offer you a bed for the night?"

"It's very kind of you, sir," said Manifold. "But if you did, I should almost certainly be late for prayers tomorrow morning. Bad for discipline."

As he walked home across the common, under the stars, he was thinking about Jock Anderson. There was, of course, a lot of sense in what he had said. It would be much more conclusive if he could catch his man actually driving the car away in a panicky effort to dispose of it. But was that his only motive? Was there something else, a suggestion of exactly the sort of sadism that Dr. Sampson had been describing to him?

Manifold knew that it was possible for a hunter to become obsessed by his quarry. He remembered meeting a man in Kenya who had started life as a game warden in India and had told him of an experience he had had when he was new at his job. A man-eating tiger had been reported in his district and he had made up his mind to kill it. It had not proved easy. Conflicting reports had been received. A number of traps had been set and he had spent long nights perched on a machan in different parts of the jungle. As failure followed failure, he had found himself beginning to credit the beast with diabolical powers and attributes. It had become a supertiger. In the end, the man said, it had fallen into a pit that some villagers had dug, and had turned out to be a mangy old tigress with very few teeth in her head; the reason, no doubt, that she had turned to man-hunting.

Wasn't that what Anderson was proposing to do? He was staking out two places and sitting over them with a gun waiting for his quarry to turn up. *And suppose, like that hunter, he was setting his traps in the wrong places?*

Manifold usually slept very well. On this occasion he was awakened by a dream. He dreamed that he knew, with complete certainty and beyond any argument, who the killer was. He said to himself, I *must* write the name down. Otherwise, when I wake up in the morning, I shall have forgotten it. Unfortunately, being at that time perched on a platform on top of a tree in the middle of the Indian jungle, he found he had neither pen nor pencil to write with.

19

Monday had not started well.

The fine weather, which had lasted almost continuously since half term, had broken. A steady, unhurried rain was coming down, with the promise of more in reserve. Gardeners and farmers might be grateful for it. Mr. Fairfax was not. A wet day meant fifty high-spirited boys confined to classrooms. The last few days of the summer term were always difficult. A number of boys were leaving, all were looking forward to the two-month break of the summer holidays. The bonds of discipline slackened.

Then the Commander had formed up after prayers and asked for the afternoon off. He said that he had a toothache, and had to visit his dentist in Guildford. Mr. Fairfax did not, precisely, disbelieve that the Commander had a toothache, but felt that it was thoughtless of him to have it at that particular moment. A well-organized member of the staff would arrange to have a toothache during the holidays.

And the telephone had started to ring.

Mr. Fairfax managed to deal, more or less rationally, with the first four mothers and two fathers who had been disturbed by their sons' Sunday letters and he was beginning to get his second wind when the telephone rang for the seventh time. It was Mrs. Busbridge. When he heard her voice, Mr. Fairfax's heart sank. Most of the parents with whom he had to deal were rational and sensible people. Where her child, Stephen, was concerned, Mrs.

Busbridge was neither rational nor sensible. She had evidently concluded from his letter that further kidnapping attempts were to be anticipated and that Stephen might be the object of one of them.

Her plan was to remove him at once, by car. She asked that his clothes be packed and that Stephen be closely guarded until she arrived.

Mr. Fairfax thought quickly. He knew that it was no good arguing with Mrs. Busbridge. He also knew that if one boy was allowed to go it might well start a panic exodus, bad in the short run and possibly even worse in the long. But he also knew that Mrs. Busbridge was in some awe of Stephen, a solemn, round-spectacled boy who exercised over her the benevolent despotism of an only child.

He said, "I think I'll get Stephen to have a word with you himself, Mrs. Busbridge. Hold the line for a moment." He then got hold of the boy and explained to him what his mother wanted. Stephen said, "It's quite all right, sir. I'll have a word with her," and advanced to the telephone. Mr. Fairfax listened unashamedly.

Stephen allowed his mother to talk for nearly a minute. Then he said, "Listen, Mum. If you take me away now, I'll never speak to you again." The telephone gave a faint squeak. Stephen repeated, "Never, do you understand? I mean it. This has been an absolutely super term. The sergeant's a policeman and another policeman arrived at half term. He's got a gun. Lots of boys have seen it. And then we had people trying to kidnap Sacher—well, I told you all about that in my letter. Some of the boys think this master shot the kidnappers. If you think I'm going to miss any of it, you can jolly well think again."

The telephone managed to get a word in. Stephen said, "Of course I shall be all right. Don't be daft." At this point the telephone evidently capitulated. Stephen, having got his way, became more affable. He said, "I expect you'll be coming down to the school play. I'll see you then. Give Topaz a big kiss from me.

Goodbye." And to Mr. Fairfax, "Topaz is my dog, sir. Rather a nice setter. Mummy's quite all right if you're firm with her."

"Yes," said Mr. Fairfax. "Yes. So I see." He went into first class feeling refreshed. The feeling lasted for ten minutes, at which point his wife put her head round the door and said, "I'm sorry to interrupt. But some reporters have arrived. I said you were busy, but they insisted on having a word with you."

"Oh, dear," said Mr. Fairfax. "All right. Write me out a translation of the rest of the exercise. You can look up any words you don't know."

He found two young men and one middle-aged woman standing about in his drawing room. Mr. Fairfax gathered that one of them represented the Chichester *Times & Journal* while the other two were the south coast representatives of London papers. He said, "There's really very little I can tell you."

"It is true that an attempt was made to kidnap Ben Sacher's son?"

"And that one of your staff was shot while defending him?"

"Not shot. No. One of them got a knock on the head."

"Could you tell us something about that?"

Mr. Fairfax gave them a brief outline of what had happened. He was conscious, as he told it, that it was a good story with a poor ending. The press evidently thought so, too.

"Can you account for these men letting the boy go?" said the lady. "It hardly seems in character."

"I'm afraid I've got no idea."

"They just drove off?"

"Apparently."

"Do you think we could have a word with the boy?"

"Certainly not. He had a considerable shock and is still under medical care."

There was an element of truth in this. Dr. Baines had prescribed a tonic for Sacher, one measured tablespoonful of which he poured down the lavatory morning and evening.

"Did his father come down to see the boy?"

"No. He spoke to him on the telephone."

When it became clear, after twenty minutes of verbal fencing, that either there was no more to the story or, if there was, they weren't going to get it from Mr. Fairfax, the three reporters departed with insincere expressions of gratitude and Mr. Fairfax thought that he had got away comparatively lightly. He was not aware that the local representative of the *Daily Express* was, at that moment, watching the first full dress rehearsal of *Twelfth Night.*

This young man had circled the school building, and coming in from the rear, had been attracted by the sound of laughter from the gym. Pushing open the side door and peering in, he thought he saw a face he recognized. "Surely," he said "it's Constance Latrobe? Wasn't it you who put on that excellent performance of the *Shrew?* Two, or was it three years ago?"

"Three and a half, actually," said Latrobe. In the handsome robes of the Duke Orsino, he was a more assured and impressive figure than in the classroom. "Who might you be?"

"Dramatic critic of the *Express,*" said the young man, improvising readily. "We heard that you were putting on a play down here. *Twelfth Night,* isn't it?" This was a tribute to his eyesight rather than his deductive powers. He had spotted a copy of the play on the table as he came in. "Your school being rather in the public eye at the moment, we thought it might be of interest to our readers if we gave them a preview of it. Could you introduce the cast, do you think?"

Nothing could have pleased Latrobe more.

It was a first-class set of costumes, which he had got hold of through a friend at the Stratford Memorial Theater. The men's clothes had needed a good deal of shortening and taking in, but the girls' dresses fitted Jared, Peter and Billy with a minimum of padding and the boys wore them with an air of unself-conscious coquetry which would have ravished the hearts of an Elizabethan audience.

"You must be Ben Sacher's son?"

"If I must be, I must be," said Jared gravely.

"That was a nasty experience you had the other night."

"I don't think—" said Latrobe.

"Quite right. Not something you'll care to remember. Who's this? Billy Warlock, of course. You're Peter Warlock's son. Your father's playing at Chichester now, isn't he?"

"He's in two of the plays," said Billy, who was used to talking to the press, and knew that they liked plenty of detail. "He's in the Anouilh and the Shaw, but not in the Pinero."

"I expect you see a good deal of him?"

"Usually only on Sundays. But he's giving a party tonight and we're going to it."

"A party?"

"It's for Peggy Lynch. She's been playing with him in both plays. She's off to America tomorrow."

"An evening party," said the reporter. "Aren't you a bit young for that?"

Billy gave him the sort of look that thirteen-year-old boys give people who make remarks of that sort, and said bleakly, "I expect we shall survive."

"Do you think I might have a photograph? If you stood together on the stage I could get you all in nicely. That's fine. You'll have to close up a little on the right. Perhaps you could put your arm round young Sacher, Mr. Latrobe? I seem to remember that she's your girlfriend in the play. Lovely."

Commander Gaze put his head round the door at this moment and said, sourly, "I hope I'm not interrupting anything. The head wants all staff in his study."

"Some of the boys," said Mr. Fairfax, "seem to have written home highly imaginative accounts of what happened when those two men broke into the school. I've been inundated with telephone calls, and have already had reporters round here. I just wanted to say that I rely on all of you to keep this thing at the lowest possible temperature. Naturally you won't talk to the press yourselves"—the Commander looked at Latrobe, who had the grace to blush—"or if you are forced to talk to them, I suggest you employ that useful formula 'No comment.' We have only ten days of term to go, and I sincerely hope we can get through it without any further disturbance."

"In a school I was at near Broadstairs," said Mr. Diplock, "we had the son of a famous racing motorist. When his father broke the world land speed record, a journalist tried to interview the boy." Mr. Diplock snuffled happily at the memory. "The headmaster chased him down the drive *with a riding crop.*"

Mr. Fairfax smiled, and said, "I hope I shan't be driven to do anything like that."

"Standing there," said the Commander, "with his arm round the boy. That'll make a nice picture, won't it? I should think the head will have a fit when he sees it."

"Publicity for the school," said Manifold.

"Not the sort of publicity a school wants. The press are only too ready to hint"—the Commander seemed to boggle at the word—"you know, homosexuality and that sort of thing."

"I know," said Manifold gravely.

"It was the same in the navy. One had to be on the lookout all the time. I remember . . ." The Commander seemed to rearrange his thoughts at the last moment and concluded, rather tamely, ". . . one or two instances. Unpleasant for all concerned."

"I suppose it was natural enough, in a way," said Manifold, wishing that he had Dr. Sampson's tape recorder with him. "Nothing but all-male company for months on end."

"That's one reason, I agree," said the Commander. "But the real trouble is lack of self-discipline. We're too soft with boys nowadays. You're not as old as I am, but you must have noticed the change, even in your lifetime. Teddy bears in bed and going out with your parents every other weekend. Look at those Warlock boys."

"What about them?"

"They've been off visiting their father and all his theatrical pals almost every weekend this term."

Manifold refrained from pointing out that if undiluted male

company was bad for a boy's morals, it must be good for him to meet the opposite sex occasionally. He said, "I shouldn't have called either of them particularly soft."

"They can play cricket," agreed the Commander. "They're probably all right at the moment. But is it going to last? They're off to a party again tonight. A *drink* party."

"I hadn't heard about that," said Manifold.

"It's some sort of theatrical do their father's giving. I think the head's been very weak about it. It's symptomatic of the way we do nothing but give in, give in." The Commander's naturally red face had become suffused by the force of his feelings.

"It's had one good side effect," said Manifold.

"Oh. What's that?"

"It seems temporarily to have cured your toothache."

The Commander looked disconcerted for a moment, and then broke out into a gruff laugh. He said, "You're quite right. And it proves my point. When you stop thinking about aches and pains they stop worrying you. Incidentally, thank you for offering to take my English class for me. Two-A. Quite a bright lot. I shall have to catch Dip and ask him to stand in for me at prep."

"You won't be back by then?"

"Not if I have to go all the way to Guildford. And this chap always keeps you waiting. I shall probably stop there and get a bite to eat afterwards."

"Always supposing you've got any teeth left to bite with," said Manifold.

Manifold had not met Two-A before, and when he came in they stared at him round-eyed as though they expected him to produce a gun and shoot out the light bulb. They were a friendly lot and it did not take long to break the ice.

He said, "What are you doing with Commander Gaze?"

Stephen Busbridge, who seemed to be the spokesman, said, "We're doing *As You Like It.* We've got to Act Four."

"And how do you do it?"

"G.G. lets us take different parts and sort of act it."

"That seems a good idea. Who takes which part?"

"We don't always do the same parts," said a redheaded boy in the back row. "No one wants to do the girls all the time."

"Then what do you do?"

"We draw for it."

Manifold cast an eye over Act Four. There seemed to be quite a few girls in it. Counting only one Lord and one Forester, he made it eight parts, which was convenient since there were eight boys. He wrote the names on eight bits of paper, folded them up, shuffled them round, and the draw took place. The only person who seemed to be disappointed in the result was a very small boy who had drawn the Forester. He said, "It's a swindle. Foresters never have anything to say."

"You're in luck this time," said Busbridge. "You've got a song to sing."

"Have I really got to sing it?"

"Of course you have. It says 'Song.' We all join in the chorus."

They threw themselves into their parts with gusto, and read them with intelligence, too, Busbridge being most suitably cast as the melancholy Jaques. Manifold realized that these were the bright boys, the ones who, next year, would be in One-A, taking the places of Sacher and McMurtrie and Joscelyne, and sitting for scholarships at public schools, and moving on and giving up their places, in turn, to another generation. One foot in youth and one foot in manhood. He felt, for the first time, the attraction that kept men like Mr. Diplock nailed to their dead-end jobs.

His mind had been straying from *As You Like It.* The flippant love scene between Orlando and the disguised Rosalind—surely a disguise that deceived no one—was bubbling merrily along.

" 'No, faith, die by attorney. The poor world is almost six thousand years old, and in all this time, there was not any man died in his own person, vid—' something. How do you pronounce it?"

"It's a sort of legal word," said Manifold cautiously. "It's usu-

187

ally spelled 'viz' nowadays. Why not say it that way."

" 'There was not any man died in his own person. Viz. in a love cause. Troilus had his brains dashed out with a Grecian club . . .' "

Manifold had once seen a head broken open by a native club, and the gray brains oozing out. It had not been a pleasant sight.

" 'But these are all lies; men have died from time to time, and worms have eaten them, but not for love.' "

The reader paused for breath. Manifold said, "Well read." The red-haired boy said, "It sounds terrific, but what does it mean, sir?"

Manifold said, "It means exactly what it says. People talk a lot of nonsense about love. They say they'll do anything for it. Sacrifice their reputations. Give up their kingdoms. Die for it, even. Shakespeare says that that's not true. People die from lots of different reasons. Cancer and coronaries and traffic accidents. But they don't die for love."

The small Forester said, "We had a pair of budgerigars. The female one got out and the cat ate her, and the male one really did pine away and die."

"Birds are more sensitive than human beings," said Manifold. "Carry on, Orlando."

The rain eased up after tea, and a watery sun came out. There was not enough heat in it to make the swimming pool attractive and Manifold decided to walk down to the village. There was a line of inquiry that he had been meaning to follow for some time, and this seemed a good chance.

Passing the front of Raybould's shop, it occurred to him that he might redeem his pledge and he went in. Mrs. Raybould shook her head. "Poor man," she said. "He seems to attract misfortune. Like a magnet. I had an elder sister; she was just the same. We all used to say if a thunderbolt fell, it'd fall on her head for sure."

"What's happened?"

"Nothing's happened yet. She's living near Bognor."

"I meant Mr. Merriam."

"It's the battery. He must have dropped it. Or dropped something on it. I said I'd see if we could patch it up, but the insulation's cracked right through." Mrs. Raybould searched under the counter and produced the battery. It certainly looked to be beyond repair.

He said, "What on earth can have happened to it?"

"You've got to face it," said Mrs. Raybould. "He's not responsible for his actions. Sooner or later he'll have to be sent somewhere where he can be looked after properly. Mrs. Loveday does her best, I'm sure. But she's not a proper nurse. There might be a very nasty accident indeed, and no one would be more sorry than Miss Shaw, who looks after him as though he was her own natural father. But she's got her work at the school."

Manifold, who had been examining the contents of his wallet, said, "How much does a new battery cost?"

"It'd be one pound forty. But seeing as how it's old Merriam . . ."

"No. That's all right," said Manifold. "I've got the money. Bit of luck on the horses. Put it on one side and I'll pick it up on my way back. I've got a job to do down the other end of the village."

Police Constable Hannaford, the local representative of the West Sussex Constabulary, lived in a large double bungalow at the far end of the village. The left-hand side housed him, his wife and his four children. The right-hand side was his official quarters. Manifold had telephoned him before he set out, and found him in his office.

Hannaford was a big, solid man, well-liked in the village, capable of turning a blind eye at the right moment but of putting down the heavy foot of the law when it seemed called for. He listened without surprise to what Manifold had to say.

"It's right," he said. "We did have one or two cases of that sort a year or so ago. How did you come to hear of it, might I ask?"

"I heard two of the boys talking about it."

"Ah, there's not much escapes them. Boys'd make good policemen. They keep their eyes and ears open and their wits about 'em."

"Could you give me the details? Times, places and so on."

"To my recollection, but I'll look in the book to make sure, we had two cases actually reported. The first was a dog. Someone had cut him open. Like it might have been one of these vivisectionists. Left him lying in the field behind Toplady's farm. Mr. Toplady was upset about that. He'd been fond of the dog. He had it put down, of course."

"Then it wasn't dead when he found it?"

"Nine parts dead, but not quite. The second one was a cat. Up in the woods behind the rectory. Strung it up and cut its paws off."

"Yes. That was the one I heard them talking about."

"It wasn't dead, either," said Hannaford. He had been looking through his station log as he spoke. "Mr. Toplady's dog, that was nearly two years ago. It was the seventh of August. The cat was the January of the year after. January the fourth. That was the day it was found."

"Yes," said Manifold. A horrible vista was opening in front of him.

"There could have been others. You find a rabbit, say, or a squirrel. And you think, poor little bugger, a dog's caught him and messed him about. So you finish him off with your boot and drop him in the ditch and think no more of it. That way, we wouldn't hear about it."

"Those were the only two that actually got reported?"

"That's right. Are the dates important?"

"Yes," said Manifold.

"You weren't thinking of a moon murderer, perhaps?"

"No. I don't think the moon comes into this."

"At the time people thought it might be Jamie Pope. He's a bit turned in his head. He wanders round talking to himself. There was a feeling he ought to be locked up. But there was no sort of proof he had anything to do with it."

"Tell me, where there any signs of a car having been parked in Toplady's field, or up in the wood where they found the cat?"

190

Hannaford looked at him curiously, and said, "Not that I remember. We didn't look into it all that closely. Thinking it was just a local boy done it. Are you tying it up with those other cases? I mean the boy at Brading and those others."

It wasn't until Hannaford said this that the sequence of events that had been slowly forming in Manifold's mind came finally into focus. He said, "I'd like you to forget that we ever had this conversation. Don't discuss it with anyone, please. Even your wife. And don't make any record of it."

When he got out into the street it was a fine evening. The last of the clouds had packed away, and the sun was smiling on a world washed clean by the rain, a world of innocent people and happy thoughts.

When a problem that has preoccupied the mind for weeks suddenly resolves itself, mixed with the satisfaction of having arrived at the solution there must always be an element of surprise, sometimes even of shock.

Manifold now found himself able to identify the face that, previously, he had seen only in his dreams. He knew, beyond logical argument, who it was who had been responsible for the maiming of animals and the deaths of boys. He could even guess what had driven him to act. There was repulsion and horror enough in the answer, but his overmastering feeling was one of sadness.

It was at six o'clock that evening, just as he was finishing his tea, that old Mr. Moritz banged his cup down with a force that nearly cracked the saucer and said, "I got it."

"God almighty," said his startled daughter. "What've you got? And whatever it is, there's no call to break our best china."

"I've remembered."

"Remembered what?"

"What it was I was trying to remember. When the police was asking me all those questions about that boy."

"All right. What was it?"

It took Mr. Moritz a minute to sort out his revelation and explain it to his daughter. She was not greatly impressed. She said, "Is that what's been worrying you all these weeks?"

"Don't you see? It's important."

"If you think it's important, you'd better tell the police. We've got that number they gave us. I wrote it down somewhere, didn't I?"

The number was eventually found, written on the back of an envelope and put away on the mantel shelf behind a photograph of the late Mrs. Moritz. The next problem was to find a telephone.

"You'd better give them a ring when you get down to the Horseshoes," said his daughter.

Mr. Moritz considered this. He wanted to watch television. It was finals day of the women's doubles at Wimbledon, and they had been promised a replay of the whole match. There was nothing he enjoyed more than seeing those nimble little girls in their short white skirts hopping about the court.

He said, "I'll go down when the tennis is finished."

"You'll be too late to catch them."

"No, I shan't," said Mr. Moritz. "You remember what that notice said. Any hour of the day or night."

It was well after half-past nine when he got to the Three Horseshoes, and it took him some time to organize himself with the necessary money and shut himself away in the little telephone booth outside the saloon. Now that it had come to the point, he felt unaccountably nervous.

A polite voice said, "Haydock Wood Special Unit. Can I help you?"

"It's about that boy who got killed. My name's Moritz." He spelled it.

"Yes, Mr. Moritz."

"I was the one who saw the car driving away." The voice at the other end sounded suddenly more interested, and said, "Would you hold on one moment, sir."

There was a pause, during which Mr. Moritz wondered if he might have to put another coin in, and then a new voice said, "Good evening, Mr. Moritz. This is Inspector Rew. I gather you've something you want to tell us?"

20

Meanwhile, in London, Detective Sergeant Michael Appleyard was chasing a memory. He was a conscientious young man. Otherwise, having been on early duty, he would, by half past four, have been in bed and asleep. Instead, he caught a trolley bus at the corner of Greys Inn Road and rolled northward in it, up the foothills of London, to Highside.

It was on Highside that he had spent his first four years as a policeman, and on its steep streets and hard pavements had worn out his first two pairs of regulation boots.

His luck was in. Sergeant Milman was still in charge of Forest Row Police Station, and was on duty when he arrived. Milman had always been a friend of his and could be relied on to give him what he wanted without wasting time asking a lot of questions. He was alone in the charge room and that was a help, too.

He said, "Hullo, young Mike. How's the dirty square mile getting along?"

"Dirtier every day," said Appleyard. "I brought along a couple of photographs I thought you might find interesting. We took 'em in a raid last week. I'll have to have them back. They're exhibits."

Sergeant Milman whistled appreciatively at the photographs and said, "The things they think of!"

"Athletic, aren't they?"

"Double-jointed, I should say. You didn't come up all this way to complete my sex education, did you?"

"Not entirely," said Appleyard. "What I brought up's another lot of photographs I wanted to show you." He spread them on the desk. "We're looking for one of these people." He explained what they were after.

Sergeant Milman had been examining the faces curiously. He said, "They all look pretty normal to me. Are you telling me one of them's a whatsit—a sort of Dr. Jekyll and Mr. Hyde? If that's right, you're more likely to spot them down in your sink of iniquity. This is a nice clean part of London, remember?"

"That's just the point," said Appleyard. "When I looked at that one, I said, straightaway, 'Highside. Promotion day.' "

"Ah," said Sergeant Milman. "Meaning that you saw it, up here, on the day you made sergeant?"

"Right."

"Then let's see what happened that day, shall we? Do you remember the date?"

"As if I should forget it! August eighteenth. Three years ago."

"I'll fetch up the book."

As Appleyard waited, in the familiar surroundings of the Forest Row charge room, every part of it connected in his mind with some episode of his early career, he was conscious of a prickle of anticipation, the radar signal that tells a policeman that he is in sight of an objective. He must be right; he knew he was right.

At first reading, the station log for August 18 proved a disappointment. None of the people who had come in that day, to ask questions, or to be asked questions, or for any of the plausible and implausible reasons that bring people into police stations, seemed to be remotely connected with the photographs on the desk. But Appleyard was not discouraged. The short, cryptic notes on the page of the book were reconstructing the day for him. The signals were coming through more and more strongly every moment.

Why had he connected it with his own promotion? Because it had been at the precise moment, when that wonderful official envelope had arrived by afternoon messenger, that he had been looking at the photograph.

Not at the original of the photograph, but at a different photograph of the same person.

The fixing of this point represented a long step forward.

He said, "Whatever it was, it happened around four o'clock in the afternoon."

"We've only got one entry at that time. 'Report of episode at Salt Lane Hospital.' "

"Salt Lane Hospital!"

Stronger and stronger.

"That's right. It was one of the doctors. He got done for bashing a patient. We didn't have to do anything about it, actually. No criminal proceedings. He just got sacked. I'm not saying there shouldn't have been. It was a nasty case. But you know what doctors are like. Never get one to give evidence against the other. Talk about the Mafia."

Appleyard wasn't really listening. He said, "There was a bit in the local paper about it, wasn't there?"

"I expect there was."

"With a photograph."

"You could be right."

"That's where I saw it, then. I'm sure of it. We were talking about that report, *and* we had the paper on the table at the time."

"Easy to check it," said Milman. "The *Gazette* will still be open. They'll turn it up for you."

At the office of the *Highside Gazette,* Appleyard explained what he wanted and an untidy young man disappeared into the basement and staggered back with a bulging folder. He said, "You'll find it here. Unless someone's pinched our file copy and not put it back. They do that sometimes, lazy bastards."

But the copy of the *Highside Gazette* for August 18 had not been removed and Appleyard unfolded its pages with hands that he tried to keep steady. It was there, on the center page. The headline said, "Outrage at Salt Lane Hospital," and the subhead, "Doctor Accused of Offenses Against Patient." The story was written in the style of qualified indignation that a newspaper employs when they are certain they are onto a good thing, but not entirely clear how far the law of libel will let them push it. Sergeant Appleyard skipped through it hastily. His eyes were on the photograph. His memory had not deceived him.

He said, "I'll want a copy of this. Several copies. Do you mind if I borrow it?"

"Help yourself," said the young man. "What's it all about? Has Dr. Lamsden got into trouble again?"

"Not exactly," said Appleyard. He folded the newspaper and slipped it into his briefcase. "I'm just going up to the hospital. Is it the same superintendent as it was when I was here? A Scotsman, with a beard."

"Dr. Mackenzie. Yes, I think he's still there."

Sergeant Appleyard took a bus up to Highside Woods and then cut across the grass to the gate on the other side which led to Salt Lane. As he walked, he was debating with himself. One side of him, the trained side, said that the information he had stumbled on was so important that it ought to be passed to the headquarters at Haydock Wood without the smallest delay. The other side, which was the human side, said, "Why not finish it? Give them the whole story. It's all there. In your pocket."

In the end he decided to compromise. The time was a quarter to seven. If the superintendent was in, and would see him, the further short delay would be justified. If not, he would get to the nearest telephone box and pass on the information he had got.

Salt Lane Hospital stood behind high, spike-topped walls in a secluded corner cut off by Highside Woods on one side and the embanked main-line railway on the other. The guardian on the gate examined Appleyard's identity card carefully before he let him through. A short walk up the laurel-lined drive brought the house in sight. It was a vast Victorian edifice, built for a city merchant. The only odd feature was that while the ground-floor windows were apparently unguarded, the windows of the three upper stories were all barred.

Luck was still running for the sergeant. Dr. Mackenzie was in and remembered him.

He said, "It was an unpleasant case. One of the most unpleasant that I can remember. And it took me by surprise. We have to be very careful when we recruit staff for a place like this. You'll understand what I mean, I'm sure."

Sergeant Appleyard nodded. He was aware of the reason for the high walls, the guarded gate and the bars on the upstairs windows. Salt Lane was one of the three North London hospitals that specialized in mental cases.

"Do I take it," said Dr. Mackenzie, "that Charles Lamsden is in trouble again? I confess I'm surprised. I would have gone bail for it that the last experience had been such a shock for him that he'd never lay hand on a patient again. When we managed to avoid bringing a charge—with the full cooperation of the authorities, may I add—we stipulated that he should never work with mentally disturbed patients again."

Sergeant Appleyard said, "I ought to have made it plain, Doctor, that it isn't Lamsden we're really interested in this time. It's the nurse."

Dr. Mackenzie's upper lip wrinkled in distaste. He said, "Yes. That was the least pleasant aspect of the whole affair. That is to say, *if* Dr. Lamsden's version is to be believed. It was never proved, you know."

"I've only got the account in the local paper to go on," said Appleyard. "It's a bit sketchy."

"It had to be. There's a law of libel, you know. More's the pity, I sometimes think. Even now, anything I tell you will have to be in confidence. I don't mean that you can't use it if it will help you in—in whatever inquiries you're now making. But if I were asked to repeat it in public, I should have to decline."

"Agreed," said Sergeant Appleyard.

He was very grateful to Dr. Mackenzie for his cooperation, but his methodical Scottish circumnavigation of the point was consuming precious minutes. It was already nearly a quarter past seven.

"Dr. Lamsden was in charge, under me, of the younger male patients. By which I mean patients between the ages of fourteen and thirty. If they are under fourteen we do not admit them. They're better off at home. He had a male assistant and three nurses to help him. We are badly understaffed, you understand, like all hospitals."

"Just like the police," said Appleyard.

"It meant long hours of duty for all concerned. And when staff are overworked it's not easy for them to show that degree of sympathy and understanding for the patients which, ideally, they should show. There was one patient in particular, a youth of nineteen, who had frequently been reported as being difficult. In an institution like this, 'difficult' has a special connotation. It does not mean that he was incontinent or unreliable. That is to be expected. It meant that he seemed to go out of his way to give extra work. Broke things. Spilled all his food on the floor, was truculent when spoken to. That sort of thing."

"And Dr. Lamsden hit him?"

"He did more than merely hit him. The evidence is that he beat him, quite systematically."

"Didn't the other patients object?"

"They didn't see it. He took him to his own room. It was only when one of the other nurses saw the marks on him, and felt bound to report it, that the facts came out."

"When you say one of the *other* nurses . . . ?"

"I mean other than the one involved. Dr. Lamsden's story, which frankly I found it a little difficult to believe, was that this nurse had incited him to these acts of cruelty. Indeed, she had done a great deal more than incite him." Dr. Mackenzie paused, and said, "You do realize that this part of the story is entirely unconfirmed."

"Yes," said Appleyard patiently.

"He alleged that she had promised him satisfaction—I will be quite explicit: I mean sexual satisfaction—if he would commit these acts of cruelty and allow her to witness them. This was, in fact, the price she was prepared to pay on each occasion."

Sergeant Appleyard took out the photographs from his brief case and laid them on Dr. Mackenzie's desk.

"And that is the nurse?" he said.

"That is Nurse Shaw," said Dr. Mackenzie.

21

As soon as Inspector Rew understood what Appleyard was trying to tell him, he said, "Hold it one moment, Sergeant. I must have this on tape. All right. Start again at the beginning and speak slowly." At the end he said, "So! Well done." Then he looked at his watch.

It was twenty minutes to eight.

The first and essential thing was to get hold of Anderson. He knew that he had been at the BBC making final arrangements for the broadcasts, which had started that evening and were to continue at six o'clock and nine o'clock every evening that week.

The obvious places were Broadcasting House, Scotland Yard and Anderson's flat. Rew tried them, unsuccessfully, and left an urgent message at each.

Next he rang Trenchard House. Lucy Fairfax answered the phone. She said she thought that Mr. Manifold was somewhere about and would fetch him. A very long pause ensued, during which Rew looked at his watch again.

In the end it was Lucy who came back to the telephone. She said crossly, "I'm sorry, Mr. Manifold isn't here. My husband tells me that he left on his motor bicycle nearly an hour ago."

"Have you any idea where he was going?"

"I think he said he was going over to see Colonel Brabazon."

"Did he say when he'd be back?"

"No," said Lucy. "He didn't. And he's meant to be on duty."

"When he does come back," said Rew, "would you please tell him to ring this number." He repeated it, giving Lucy time to write it down.

"*If* I am still about when he comes back," said Lucy crossly, "I will pass on the message."

"I'd be much obliged if you would," said Rew. "It really is extremely important."

Next he tried Colonel Brabazon, and there he found Manifold. He said, "Something has turned up here, Ken. I can't very well discuss it on the telephone. I'm trying to locate Jock, who seems to have disappeared. As soon as I can get him, he's bound to want you."

"Understood," said Manifold. "I'd better come right over. I wanted to see him anyway. I've got onto something at this end which might be helpful. Be with you in about forty-five minutes."

It was a quarter to nine when a car drew up in the street outside the Haydock Wood police hut, immediately followed by a motorbike. Anderson and Manifold came into the hut together.

Anderson said, "I hear you've been chasing me, David. Central found me at my sister's flat. I was having dinner there. What's up?"

"I'd like you to listen to this," said Rew.

The quiet voice of Sergeant Appleyard filled the hut. The man who was writing up the night's log stopped writing. The duty telephonist took off his headset to listen. Everyone listened. Manifold thought it was like the final movement of a long and complex musical work, the artful arrangement of notes that sums up and explains everything that has gone before.

There was a click as the recording finished, and a moment of silence.

Then Anderson said, "What a bitch. What a bloody—awful—filthy—bitch. I suppose she caught Warr the same way."

"That's right," said Manifold. "She started him off torturing animals. I was going to tell you about that. Then, when he was well and truly hooked, it went on with boys. Every time, the same payoff. He satisfied her sadism. She satisfied him with sex. A horrible cold-blooded bargain."

Anderson said, "Our real mistake was over the scientific evidence. Not that it was wrong. We just read it wrong. They said there was no sign of a second person on the scene. Of course there wasn't. That bitch stayed in the car. She wasn't interested in *doing* things. Her kick was watching them. That's clear from the evidence of what happened at the hospital."

"I imagine that's how she got away with it on that occasion," said Manifold. "Her story would be that the doctor ordered her to be there. *She* took no part in what went on. She was just a spectator. She was as shocked as anyone else, but after all, the doctor was in charge, wasn't he? She had to do what she was told, didn't she? The authorities mayn't have believed her, but they couldn't prove anything. They got rid of her, but they had to give her a reasonable chit when she went on to the next place. She seems to have behaved herself there."

While Manifold had been talking, Anderson had been thinking. He said, "It was a perfect setup. She'd drive the car. He'd be hiding in the back. A boy who was in a hurry wouldn't think twice about accepting a lift from a girl by herself. Once the boy was safely in, Warr would grab him, pull him over into the back and tie him up. Then he'd take over driving. He'd be wearing glasses and a white wig in case anyone happened to spot him. She'd be in the back, keeping an eye on the boy."

"I imagine that's how it developed," said Manifold. "The first case may have been a bit more impromptu. There's a suggestion in the report that Fenton was mentally retarded. They may have seen him wandering along the road, and picked him up on the spur of the moment. The second and third cases were carefully planned. No doubt about that."

"So that's the truth of the matter," said Anderson. A thought occurred to him. "What brought you here, Ken? Has there been some development at your end?"

"Not really a development," said Manifold. "It was just that I'd come to the same conclusion as Sergeant Appleyard, but by a different route. It was the local bobby talking about the cases of animal maiming. As soon as I tried to fit it into the pattern of the case, I realized that it *must* be Warr or the girl. Probably both of them."

"Why?"

"Because both the animal maiming cases took place during the school holidays. The rest of the staff would have been miles away. And we knew the Fairfaxes were out of it."

"Yes, I see," said Anderson.

He said it absently. The long run-up was finished. His mind was groping ahead, planning the final stage of the campaign: the last and most difficult stage, when you knew who the criminal was; when you knew that you would have to stand up, months later, in court, and prove it; a stage where every step you took and every word you said would be subject to cross-examination, and where a single mistake might wipe out all the gains you had made.

He was still thinking when the telephone rang.

Constable Toft lifted the receiver, listened for a moment, and said to Manifold, "It's for you, sir. From the school."

22

"One of the kids," said Sacher, "was listening on his transistor, when he ought to have been doing his prep. He said that there was a police notice about that boy."

"Which boy?" said McMurtrie lazily. The three of them were sitting in their customary places on the edge of Joscelyne's bed, watching another July evening fade into dusk.

"The one who was tortured and killed."

"Lister," said Joscelyne. "I remember the name."

"What did it say?"

"The police are looking for a dark-gray BMC four-door saloon, about ten years old, with a plug in the nearside rear tire. The search is being concentrated in an area northeast of Chichester."

"We're northeast of Chichester," said McMurtrie thoughtfully.

"So are a billion other places," said Joscelyne.

"What are you thinking about?" said Sacher.

"I was wondering about our Mr. Manifold. You know when you heard Brab telling T.E.F. that Manifold was nothing to do with keeping an eye on you. Why should he have said that? He knew jolly well that Manifold was a policeman."

"He didn't want T.E.F. to get into a flap."

"Possibly. *But suppose that Manifold came here on a different line altogether.* Something he didn't want to tell T.E.F. about."

"You mean," said Sacher slowly, "that one of the staff here might be the man the police are after for that job."

"Why not? It happened at half term. They haven't got an alibi between them."

The three boys thought, though not very seriously, about the possibility of one of their masters being a torturer and a killer.

"If I had to pick one of them," said Sacher, "it'd be G.G."

"Why?"

"He's obviously up to something. Slipping out every night after dark."

"He hasn't got a BMC with a plug in its tire."

"He might have a spare car," said Sacher. "Somewhere out on the common."

"Sounds a bit far-fetched to me," said Joscelyne.

Outside the owl hooted twice, as if in agreement.

McMurtrie said, "Only ten days more. Are you sorry?"

"Not a scrap," said Sacher.

"I am, a bit," said Joscelyne with a sigh. "We've got pretty well dug in here. I don't much want to move."

"I can't make my mind up," said McMurtrie. "I've enjoyed it here. This term particularly. But I've got a feeling it's time to move on."

"You'll be a beastly little fag," said Sacher. "Cleaning out the prefects' porridge saucepans and blacking their boots. You ought to come out to Israel with me. They take education seriously there. They don't pretend it's something out of the *Boys' Own Paper.*"

"Won't you be scared? Someone else might take a shot at you."

Jared considered the matter. He said, "I don't think being killed unexpectedly is a thing to be frightened about. You don't know anything about it until it happens and after it's happened you don't know anything about it either. Suppose, for instance, you were going to be killed tonight."

"Thank you."

"No, I mean it. It could happen. A branch from an elm tree could fall on your head. Or a poacher, out after rabbits, could blaze off, not knowing you were the other side of the hedge, or a car traveling without lights could knock you down as you were nipping across the road—"

"If you don't shut up," said McMurtrie, "I shan't go at all. Cars. Elm trees. Poachers."

"Well, you won't get caught by the staff, anyway," said Joscelyne. "Our Mr. Manifold has buzzed off somewhere on his motorbike. G.G.'s in Guildford having a tooth out, or so he says. Probably at a pub. Connie's boozing with the Warlock crowd. Nigel's down in the village with his girlfriend. And it's T.E.F.'s night for bridge with the vicar. The only one left is old Dip, and he's deep in the *Times* crossword puzzle."

"I don't know what our parents pay fees for," said Sacher. "Fifty boys and only one Dip to look after them. What would happen if a fire broke out?"

McMurtrie had pulled on trousers and a sweater over his pajamas, and was now lacing up his gym shoes. He said, "I'll be back in about a quarter of an hour."

After he had gone, Sacher sat for so long in silence that Joscelyne said, "What's wrong?"

"It's silly," said Sacher. "But I suddenly thought, Suppose what I said was right. I mean, about him being killed. I wish I hadn't said it."

McMurtrie had planned a route that would keep him out of trouble. To cross in front of the house was dangerous. Too many hostile windows. He would use the side door, cross the lawn and make a circuit through the kitchen garden and orchard. This was to deal with the possibility that Mr. Diplock would be in the staff common room. If he was there, he was unlikely to be looking out of the window, but old Dip was unpredictable. From the orchard he could make his way back into the park; from that point he would be on his daytime route.

His hand was actually on the handle of the side door when he heard the car. It came racing down the drive, swung round the corner and stopped with a squealing of brakes. The headlights showed for a moment under the door. Then the car ground its gears, backed and came forward again on a different tack. So. It was being put away in the staff garage.

McMurtrie opened the nearest door, which led into a classroom, and closed it, leaving a crack to see through. A minute later the side door opened with a crash and the Commander surged into the passage. He was humming to himself and walking with a more than nautical roll.

"Pissed as a newt," said McMurtrie, as he watched him tack down the passage and disappear round the corner. He tiptoed out through the side door, which the Commander had left wide open, across the path, and onto the lawn. Here he took to his heels and ran, pausing only when he had reached the tangled safety of the sunken garden.

It was a perfect night. A dying moon hung in the sky. The stars were beginning to show, and a light breeze, which was hardly a wind, more a movement of the air over the cooling earth, brought with it the mixed smells of summer. What a night, thought McMurtrie. What a night to be out in the open and on the move. What a night to be alive in.

Following his chosen path, he crossed the kitchen garden, circled back into the park and squeezed out through the railings onto the side road. He was crouching in the ditch when he heard a great rattling noise. Two bicycles came belting down the road within inches of his nose. Neither was carrying any sort of light. The first was ridden by a girl. The second, in pursuit, by a boy. The girl gave a shriek as she went past. The boy screamed back. McMurtrie grinned to himself. Being cut down by amorous bicyclists was one fate that Sacher had left out of his catalogue of deaths.

When he walked into the wood yard, he found Mr. Bishop sitting on a chair in front of his own door and smoking a pipe.

"Fancied you might have had second thoughts, young Mac," he said.

"Certainly not, your right reverence. And I've got the money.

One pound fifty for the vodka and sixteen pence for the two bottles of bitter lemon you let us have on Saturday."

"Bang on the nail," said Mr. Bishop. Bottle and money changed hands. "You want to go slow with this stuff. It's strong medicine."

McMurtrie said, "If we all got stinking, we should only be following the example of our pastors and masters." He told him about his encounter with the Commander.

"Shocking," said Mr. Bishop. "You'd better be getting back before someone misses you."

It was as he said this that they heard more than one set of footsteps coming down the lane, and recognized a well-known voice.

Mr. Fairfax had not been able to give more than half his mind to his bridge. His opponents, who were the vicar and his wife, and his partner, who was Dr. Baines, were all serious players. When Mr. Fairfax had first called out of turn and then revoked twice, in consecutive hands, he apologized and threw in the sponge.

"I'm terribly sorry," he said. "But I'll have to call it a day. I've had to leave the school almost unattended. Mr. Diplock's meant to be on duty, but he's perfectly capable of forgetting all about it and pottering off down to the village."

"Once he'd got his nose down in one of those photographic magazines of his," said Dr. Baines, "old Dip wouldn't notice if a bomb went off."

"Please don't talk about bombs," said the vicar's wife faintly.

"In the ordinary way, I wouldn't mind," said Mr. Fairfax. "But in the light of some of the things that have happened this term . . ."

"We quite understand," said the vicar.

"In any event," said Dr. Baines, "if you had revoked a third time I should have been forced to ask you to pay my losses. I have a letter to post. I'll walk with you as far as the main road."

When McMurtrie heard his headmaster's voice he acted quickly. The half bottle of vodka was thrust back into Mr. Bishop's hand, and he was across the yard in a flash. There was an open shed on the far side, full of balks of timber, which would, he reckoned, give him cover. He stepped back into its shadow.

The footsteps came to a halt. Mr. Fairfax said, "Why, it's Mr. Bishop. Enjoying this lovely evening, I expect. Lucky I saw you. I was meaning to have a word with you."

McMurtrie looked round. His hiding place would have served well enough if T.E.F. had simply been passing down the road. If, blast the man, he was going to settle down in the yard for a long natter, something more permanent would have to be found. He edged his way in, stepping over the clutter on the floor, toward the storehouse at the back.

The first thing he saw was a ladder, leading up to a trap door in the roof. Excellent. He would climb it.

"Wednesday will be all right," he heard Mr. Fairfax say. "But we may have to cancel Saturday. Most of your regulars are involved in the play and will be rehearsing."

The trap door led to a loft. McMurtrie squeezed through and sat down. Now that he was safe he was ready to enjoy the situation. Below him, the talk droned on. There was a third voice, which he recognized as belonging to the school doctor. At last it came to an end, and he heard two pairs of footsteps tiptapping away up the road. Give them five minutes, he thought. Then nip back quick.

He felt in his right-hand trouser pocket for the pencil flashlight that he always carried there, and clicked it on. He was in a sort of tunnel, floored with stacked planks and roofed with tiles. The far end was a triangle of darkness. He crawled along to investigate.

When he got there he saw that the building he was in and the one next to it must originally have been a single structure. A wall had been run up to cut it into two, but it had not been thought worthwhile to carry it up to the roof. The triangle at the end was an opening, leading into the other section.

He peered through.

Immediately below him, its curved top reflecting the light he directed down, stood a dark-gray four-door saloon car. He put the flashlight back in his pocket, turned over onto his stomach and propelled himself backward. The opening was not large, but it was large enough. His feet touched the top of the car, which cracked in protest under his weight. He stepped down from it onto the hood, and then onto the floor.

It was while he was fumbling for his flashlight that the full meaning of what he had done struck him for the first time. Suppose that the fantasy they had been discussing in the dormitory less than half an hour before was true. Suppose this was the very car the police were looking for. Suppose the doors leading out to the road were locked. He had got in. Was he going to get out again? If he shouted, could Mr. Bishop hear him?

He had the flashlight in his hand now, and clicked it on. The plug in the nearside rear tire was chillingly plain.

At that moment his heart gave a jump and seemed to turn right over. Someone was coming up the road. Someone who was walking softly, but quickly. Someone who had now stopped outside the door.

McMurtrie had one thought only, and that was to hide. He squeezed himself between the side of the car and the wall.

A key grated in the lock, and one of the double doors swung open. Someone was coming into the garage. Were they going to turn the light on? No. The footsteps came round to the side of the car where McMurtrie was crouching. Then the opening of the nearside door turned on the light inside the car.

McMurtrie heard a gasp of surprise, and knew that he had been spotted. As he started to get up, a soft arm whipped round his throat from behind. He struggled furiously against it, but his body and legs were trapped.

The pressure increased.

A soft voice said, "Well, well. A little spy."

McMurtrie tried to shout, but the merciless pressure on his windpipe prevented him.

"Only one possible sentence for spies," said the voice. "Death."

"Death" was the last word he heard.

Mr. Bishop also had decided to give Mr. Fairfax five minutes to get away. His conscience in the matter of the vodka was far from clear. At the end of this time he went across to the storehouse and called the boy's name softly.

When he got no answer, it occurred to him that McMurtrie must have wriggled out of the window at the far end and be already on his way back to school. He smiled at the memory of the tense moment when they had heard Mr. Fairfax's voice, and the smile was still on his lips when he went indoors and saw the half bottle of vodka standing on the table where he had put it down.

Odd! Surely the boy would not have gone away and left it behind.

Mr. Bishop walked out again into the yard. He was puzzled and uneasy. At this moment he heard a car start up in the garage next door.

He stepped out into the road.

The car was backing out of the garage. To make the turn, it had to swing left-handed, and this brought its rear windows directly into Mr. Bishop's view.

There was a bundle on the back seat, covered by a rug. From one corner of the bundle what looked like a gym shoe was sticking out. The car finished reversing and moved off down the lane.

Mr. Bishop stood for a moment, staring after it. Then he went back into his house, fetched a big flashlight, trotted across with it to the storehouse and started to search. His first idea, that McMurtrie might have escaped by the window, was soon proved wrong. The only window was tightly shut and laced with old spiderwebs.

The other possibility was the ladder. Mr. Bishop climbed it and squeezed his head and shoulders through the trap door. Marks in the dust showed him that he was on the right track. He hoisted himself through the opening and crawled to the triangle of darkness at the end. The strong beam of his light showed him that the garage was empty.

It showed him something else.

Lying on the floor, beside the door, was a silver pencil flashlight which he recognized.

It took him a minute to extract himself from the loft and less than a minute to reach the call box on the corner. It was Lucy Fairfax who answered the telephone. She said, "Yes. My husband's just got back."

Mr. Bishop said, "Please, Mrs. Fairfax. Fetch him. Quickly, please. It's urgent."

It says something for the events through which they had lived that term that Lucy did not stop to argue. Mr. Fairfax was at the telephone in less than a minute. Mr. Bishop poured out his story, speculation and fact tripping over each other in his haste.

Mr. Fairfax said, "Go straight round to the police station. Quicker to go yourself than to ring. Tell them you think you've seen the car which was in the broadcast this evening. That's all. They'll know what to do." To Lucy he said, "Run up quickly, and check that McMurtrie hasn't come back."

As Lucy was going, she remembered something. She said, "A man telephoned for Ken Manifold earlier this evening. I think he was a policeman. He gave me this number."

By the time she came running back with the news that McMurtrie's bed was empty, Mr. Fairfax was speaking to the police headquarters at Haydock Wood.

23

As soon as Manifold grasped what was being said, he made a sign to Constable Toft, who switched the call onto retransmit. Then they could all hear Mr. Fairfax's voice. The horror in it was magnified by the transmission and filled the room.

"Timings," said Anderson. "We *must* have timings."

Manifold put the question. They could sense Mr. Fairfax trying to pull himself together and consider the matter calmly. He said, "It wasn't more than five minutes ago when Bishop telephoned me. And from what he told me, it might have taken him ten minutes to realize the boy was gone and get to the call box."

"Good enough," said Anderson. He had moved over to the table map. "That girl went to the garage to fetch the car. Then she drove it round to the house to pick up Warr. They were planning to dump it."

He sat in a chair at the head of the table and pressed one of the three selector switches.

"That's right," said Manifold. "They heard the six o'clock announcement, and it bolted them."

"But they weren't expecting the boy. That must have held them up for a minute or two." He started to dial numbers. "They can't be more than ten minutes gone. Probably less." Then, into his handset, "Control. Alert all watchers. This is the car we described to you last week. It's moving northeast from map square 2496. Repeat, 2496. It will now be from three to six miles from its starting place. Acknowledge."

On the map, points of light were already starting to appear. Manifold saw that they formed three rough arcs. The inner arc made a ring round Chichester, seven to ten miles from it. Petersfield, Rogate, Trotton, Midhurst, Petworth, Pulborough, Storrington and Arundel. The lights were not in the villages themselves but at points near them, often at crossroads. Two of them were at level crossings and two were on bridges over the Rother.

Anderson had broken into a flow of coded signals to Control. "Easy Fox two three. George two three. Item King three three owe. Check. Cancel three three owe. Three three one. Love Mike three three two."

The sweat was standing out in a band across his forehead as he concentrated the whole of his mind on the game of blindfold chess that he was playing across the board of the English countryside.

Manifold had been aware for some minutes that Rew was taking a call on one of the other telephones. He saw him hesitate. Then, as though he had made his mind up, he climbed to his feet and moved quickly across. He tapped Anderson on the shoulder.

For a moment Manifold thought Anderson was going to hit him. Then the discipline of experience took control. He even managed to smile as he said, "Well, David, what is it?"

"Mr. Moritz has just come through. He's remembered that when he saw the car driving away that night there was some defect in the rear light which made it flicker on and off. Just like the Morse code, he said."

Anderson grabbed the transmitter and said, "All watchers. Add to description of car. The taillight is defective. I repeat, the taillight is defective and will be seen to flicker. Thank you, David. That should clinch it."

It will clinch it, thought Manifold, if we're right about one point. That they've gone inland. It was a fair assumption. Inland was their customary stalking ground. It was the area they knew best. But on this occasion they weren't looking for a victim. They had a car and a body to dispose of. Suppose they were heading in the opposite direction, southwest? There was no point in saying any of this to Anderson. He was using the only apparatus that was available to him, and using it well. But there was no burking the fact that it only covered half the ground.

More lights were springing up. This was a second ring. Liphook, Kingsley Green, Blackdown, Balls Cross, Adversane, Ashington. Reports were coming in, too, none of them good enough for a definite identification. Anderson had a board beside him, covered with gridded paper, which reproduced the map squares in the area he was searching. As a "possible" was announced, he repeated the coordinates to an assistant, who marked the board with small blue-headed pins. Presently a pattern started to form; a pattern of cars, moving through the dusk, watched by unseen eyes, their courses plotted.

Anderson looked at his watch. Nearly fifteen minutes had gone since he had set the machinery into motion.

"Come on," he said softly. "For Christ's sake, come on."

It was a prayer, and like a prayer it was answered.

A red light showed on the board at the crossroads a hundred yards east of Trotton. Anderson listened, and then repeated, "Definite identification. A four-door dark-gray saloon car, heading north, with a defective rear light. The driver thought to be a man with white hair and glasses. Mark it in."

He suddenly sounded ten years younger. "David, get the standby car from Petersfield moving east toward Woodmansgreen, and one from Haslemere coming south through Fernhurst. Keep both cars on your net. Reports to you every three minutes, negative as well as positive."

Looking at the map, Manifold could see that the car they were after was moving into a triangle formed by the A-3, the A-286 and the B-272. With a line of watchers behind and in front, and two cars beating the coverts, surely, surely they couldn't slip out now.

Sacher and Joscelyne were sitting up in bed, staring at each other. Lucy Fairfax had arrived and gone in a flurry of footsteps.

Joscelyne said, "Why did you tell her?"

Sacher stared at him.

"Why did you tell her where he went? Couldn't you have said he'd gone to the lavatory, or something?"

"What would have been the point of it?"

"It would have stalled her."

Sacher said, "After all that's happened this term, Peter, if you still can't see where reality breaks in, it's time you made the effort and grew up."

After which pronouncement he lay down, turned over in bed, and not another word could Joscelyne get out of him through that long and horrible night.

While they were waiting, Manifold used one of the outside lines to telephone the school. He said to Mr. Fairfax, "No. Nothing definite yet, but we think we'll be able to head them off all right. There's something you could do, if you would."

It was clear that Mr. Fairfax would do anything to relieve the strain of waiting.

"Go down and have a word with old Mr. Merriam. Ask him if the car that was kept in the shed at the bottom of the garden belonged to him."

"I seem to remember that it did," said Mr. Fairfax. "He laid it up about three years ago, when he had his stroke."

"Make him write down the registration number and phone me back here, as quick as you can. Use the phone box at the end of the lane."

Rew said, "What made you think of that all of a sudden?"

"I ought to have worked it out a long time ago," said Manifold bitterly. "It was so bloody obvious. That's why they busted up the old boy's wireless set and battery. They knew the description of the car would be broadcast sooner or later. And of course if it was his car, he'd have recognized it."

"The number, it'll be useful. But not as useful as that bit about the taillight."

"God bless Mr. Moritz," said Manifold.

"Car one negative," said Rew. And a moment later, "Car two negative."

"What the hell are they up to?" said Anderson. "They crossed at Trotton ten minutes ago. They must be up to the next line by now."

If they get there, thought Manifold. The same thought was in everybody's mind, but it remained unspoken. He could see the car turning down a side lane, and then into a field; the bundle at the back which was McMurtrie rolled out onto the grass.

"Car one negative. Car two negative."

Anderson said, "What other cars have we got, David?"

"Two at Horsham on immediate call. Two at Crawley on fifteen minutes notice."

"Get one of the Horsham cars into the area. Tell it to move laterally, in a slow sweep between Lickfold and Borden. And put the Crawley cars on notice now."

"Car one negative. Car two negative."

Manifold knew exactly what Anderson wanted to do. He wanted to jump into his own car and drive at top speed into the countryside north of Trotton; to thrash round and search every likely corner for the car which he knew must be there. And the moment he did so, all real control would be lost. It was the same training that let him smile and talk quietly to Rew that kept him anchored to his post when all his human instincts were urging him to leave it.

"Car three moving west now," said Rew.

The outside telephone rang. It was Mr. Fairfax. He sounded breathless. He said, "I've got the number for you. GKM 702 C."

Manifold wrote it down and put the paper on the table beside Anderson; who looked at it, nodded and started passing the number into the set.

"Car one negative. Car two negative." Pause. "Car three has reached search area."

The assistant commissioner for Metropolitan Police spoke on the telephone to Sir Charles McMurtrie, who had been located at a dinner at the Mansion House. Sir Charles listened in silence.

Then he said, "Thank you for taking the trouble to telephone. I will make my excuses and go back to my flat. You have the number, I think? I'll wait there for news."

When he had rung off, he stood for a moment, thinking. His first thought was for his wife, who was at their country cottage, and probably on the point of going to bed. Should he ring her up now, or wait for more definite news? He thought it would be kinder to wait.

Then he thought about what Mr. Fairfax had said: "a very balanced boy. One of the best . . ."

Alastair McMurtrie opened his eyes.

The first things he was conscious of was a burning pain in his throat, and then a beating of blood in his ears.

The next thing he noticed, a few inches away from his eyes, was a female ankle. Then he remembered everything, and the sweat started out all over his body.

He was lying on the floor of a car, which was traveling quite slowly along a bumpy road. Above his head an argument was going on. He recognized both the voices. This added to the horror.

The sleeves of his sweater had been pulled down tight over his hands and knotted together, producing the effect of a strait jacket. He could move his arms a few inches up and down, but no effort he could make was going to bring them round from behind his back.

The car had stopped, and the conversation became more urgent. As the driver leaned back to say something, McMurtrie saw that it was indeed Nigel Warr, but a parody of his everyday self. He was wearing a fluffy white wig and a pair of steel-rimmed glasses. The effect was so grotesque that it seemed to him, in a moment of wild relief, that it must be a nightmare. If only he could jerk free of it, he would wake up and find himself back in his bed in dormitory.

The movement he made attracted attention.

"Young master Alastair has woken up," said Elizabeth. "Shall I put him to sleep again?"

"Leave him alone," said Nigel. He spoke in an odd high-pitched voice, quite unlike his normal tones. "He won't make any trouble now."

Elizabeth looked down at the bundle at her feet. She said, in a cooing voice, "Were you planning to make trouble, young master Alastair?"

McMurtrie tried to speak, and realized for the first time that there was a broad strip of sticking plaster sealing his mouth.

He shook his head violently.

"That's very wise of you," said Elizabeth. "An old head, one might say, on young shoulders. Because *if* you gave the slightest sign of wanting to cause any trouble, it would be terribly tempting, and really quite simple, to stop it—like this."

She leaned down and very deliberately pinched McMurtrie's nostrils between forefinger and thumb. After a few seconds he started to fight wildly and blindly for air. Wedged as he was in the space behind the back seat, the limit of what he could do was to arch his body and shake his head, trying to shift the hand from his face.

Elizabeth laughed, and put one foot on his body, pressing it down, but without relaxing her hold.

There was a bursting agony in McMurtrie's chest, a red mist behind his eyes and a drumming of blood in his ears. Then the fingers were loosened and he started to suck air back through his nostrils, into his lungs.

"That's all right, then," said Elizabeth. "I'm sure he'll be good."

The tears were streaming down the boy's face.

"Car one negative. Car two negative. Car three negative."

"Where the hell can they have got to?" said Anderson. No one answered him. They had been waiting twenty-five intolerable minutes for a sighting.

220

Anderson said, "How many more cars have we got?"

"One more at Horsham," said Rew, "and the two at Crawley should be ready by now."

"All right," said Anderson. "Tell them—" He stopped. A red light had come up. He listened, and said, "Definite identification. Four-door dark-gray saloon GKM 702 C, with defective rear light. Observed crossing A-29 one hundred yards north of Adversane. Adversane! What the hell . . ."

All eyes switched to the map.

Anderson said, "If he crossed the B-272 near Trotton, how the devil did he get there? It doesn't make sense."

Manifold said, "It makes sense if he's making for a definite objective."

"Come again."

"If he was just driving blindly into the countryside, looking for the first lonely wood or quarry to dump the car in, he certainly wouldn't go to Adversane via Trotton. But if he's making for a specific location beyond Adversane, it's quite possible he missed his way early on. He'd be sticking to minor roads and map reading at night isn't all that easy. When he gets to Trotton he sees from the signpost that he's wrong and switches course due east —still keeping to small roads and tracks. That would bring him where he is now, and the timing would be right, too."

Anderson grunted agreement. "It's bringing him damned close to us," he said. "If he keeps straight on, he could be within a couple of miles of this place in ten minutes. Switch all the cars into this area, David. Tell the Crawley pair they can start now, and drive slowly towards us."

It gave them all an uncanny feeling, the thought that the invisible car, which they had been pursuing with lights and signals across a map, should be driving toward them; that it might actually materialize in the street outside.

"Rudgwick, Rowhook, Broadbridge Heath," said Anderson. "Specially alert, please. The notified car may be in your area any moment now."

"Crawley are moving," said Rew.

It was at this point in the proceedings that Constable Toft coughed. It was the sort of cough that invited attention. Everyone looked at him. He said, "Chuckston Pool?" The constable on the telephone exchange nodded vigorous agreement. They were both local men.

"What about it?" said Anderson.

"It's very deep," said Toft. "They say no one's ever really found the bottom. Part of an old clay pit, but there're mine galleries underneath it."

"You put that car into Chuckston Pool," said the second constable, "you'd never see it again. Never. There's a scour at the bottom. Carry it along."

"Point it out," said Anderson.

Toft put his finger on a small blue circle on the map. As he did so a red light came up. It was almost exactly halfway between the second red light and the pool.

"Coneyhurst Common. Definite identification. I think you're right, Toft. I'm going to back your hunch, anyway. Three cars concentrate on that point, David. When they get close, they're to run on side lights only. The Crawley contingent can act as backstop. You take charge. I'm going out. Toft, come with me to show my driver the way."

Manifold said, "Room for me?"

Anderson nodded. They piled into the car and swung off down the street.

"Turn left here," said Elizabeth. "Quite a small lane, and it's pretty steep. You'll need bottom gear. That's it. There used to be a gate at the top, but it isn't always shut."

The gate was open, and the car drove out onto a stretch of springy turf. Ahead of them a white-painted post and rail fence showed in their headlights.

Nigel swung the car so that it pointed back toward the gate, switched off all the lights, and they were in the glimmering dusk of a summer night.

They had come out onto a grassy plateau. All around them, in the middle distance, they could see the scattered lights of houses, and in the far distance a stream of headlights on the A-29. Where they were it was quiet and private.

When Nigel spoke, his voice sounded as if it was being forced out of him under pressure. He said, "And what do you suggest we do now?"

"Plenty of time," said Elizabeth lazily. "It'll take us less than half an hour to walk to Billingshurst. No risk of losing the last train. Pull the boy out."

Nigel lifted McMurtrie out and laid him down on the turf. He had taken his glasses off, and his wig had slipped to one side. He stared down blankly at McMurtrie and McMurtrie stared back at him. There was a long silence.

Elizabeth said, "Well, well. When does the show start?"

"It doesn't," said Nigel. "We put him back in the car and push it over the edge. That's all."

"No show, no sweets," said Elizabeth.

She was sitting on the back seat of the car, with the door wide open. She looked like a little girl at the pantomime perched on the edge of her seat waiting for the curtain to go up.

It was at that moment, and without warning, that she moved. She pulled the car door shut, slid over into the driver's seat, started the car and drove straight through the gate.

Nigel stood for a moment, staring at the winking rearlight of the car as it bucketed down the lane. Then he saw what Elizabeth had seen a few seconds earlier. Two cars, showing side lights only, were coming up the road they had followed. He could see something else. A third car, previously hidden, was coming from the opposite direction.

As Elizabeth reached the road, she swung left, and accelerated. It was only when she rounded the curve in the road that she saw the car ahead of her. It was far too late to stop. The cars met, head on, in a splintering explosion of sound.

Anderson's car was first up the track, and Manifold had tumbled out before it stopped.

Nigel had crouched down, on his knees, beside McMurtrie. Anderson shouted something, and Manifold said, "The boy's all right." He fumbled for a moment with the knotted sleeves, and then lost patience and ripped the sweater right off, over McMurtrie's head, and pulled it down clear of his arms.

The second car had arrived and there were half a dozen men on the scene. They were crowded round the kneeling Nigel, but seemed uncertain what to do.

Anderson said, "Get a rug round the boy. We don't want him dying of cold." And nodding down at Nigel, "Put that thing into the car."

When the first hands touched him, Nigel started to scream, on a thin, high-pitched note, like a child in agony. His body had gone completely rigid.

One of the men said, "He isn't cooperating, sir."

"Lift him and sling him in."

Two men picked Nigel up, still in a kneeling position, and still screaming, and put him in the back of the car.

McMurtrie was on his feet by now. One of the policemen had put a blanket around his shoulders, and he was trying to control his shivering.

Anderson said, "Take that thing to Horsham. I'll be there myself as soon as I've found out what the damage was down there. You'd better take care of the boy, Ken. You can use the second car. If you think he ought to go to hospital . . . I'll leave that to you."

Manifold said, "He'll be better off in his own bed at school, I guess," and McMurtrie nodded his head vigorously. He seemed to be recovering.

As the driver of the second car was turning it, preparing to go, Manifold stood, for a moment, by himself at the railing, looking down at the sheet of water below. Black as ink, it reflected no stars.

"And men have died," he said to himself. "And worms have eaten them. But *not* for love."

24

"So Elizabeth is dead," said Mr. Fairfax.

"God, yes," said Manifold. "She's dead. The cars met head on, both going fast. The policemen were bruised and shocked, but they did have their seat belts on. Elizabeth didn't. She went through the windscreen, face first."

It was still only a few minutes after midnight. McMurtrie was asleep in his room. Manifold was drinking a mug of coffee in the Fairfaxes' sitting room and trying to stop yawning.

"Do you think he'll be all right?" said Lucy.

Manifold guessed that she meant McMurtrie. He said, "I should think so. He hardly stopped talking all the way home."

"What about Warr?" said Mr. Fairfax.

"It all depends," said Manifold. He didn't want to talk about Nigel. He needed a night's rest to blur the memory of that crouched and screaming creature.

He said, "I imagine that someone like Dr. Sampson will have to decide. If he isn't fit to plead, there can't be any proceedings."

"I'm sorry if it sounds brutal," said Mr. Fairfax, "but for the sake of the school I can only pray that he never recovers."

Lucy said, in her level, husky voice, "Poor Nigel. I always knew she'd destroy him. Much better for him if he doesn't recover. It's Elizabeth I'm sorry about."

"Sorry?" said Mr. Fairfax.

"I'm sorry she's dead. I should have preferred it to be the other way round. Nigel dead and that woman facing fifteen or twenty years in prison. I believe the other prisoners take it out of someone who's been convicted of hurting children, don't they? That way she'd have suffered for all the suffering she's caused."

Manifold looked at her curiously. A strange woman, moved by strange tides. He said, "I'm going to bed. I've told McMurtrie to keep his mouth shut. You'd better warn Sacher and Joscelyne in the morning. The less they say about all this the better."

"The less *anyone* says about it the better," said Mr. Fairfax.

"Of course he isn't fit to plead," said Dr. Sampson.

"I suppose what finished him," said Manifold, "was the girl running out on him in that cold-blooded way, leaving him to face the music."

"Nothing of the sort. What destroyed him was guilt. A stronger dissolvent than any acid known to science. Think about it. Here was a very ordinary young man, brought up between the normal signposts of right and wrong. Then think about the price he was forced to pay for that woman. First he had to tie up small animals and torment them for her amusement. Then it was boys. All right, they were strange boys, picked up casually. But then fate played him a deadly trick. This time it was a boy he had taught, a boy he knew and liked. That showed him what he was doing. Showed it in plain black and white and finished him off as quickly and as brutally as a boot on the head."

Manifold thought about it. He said, "It's pretty clear that he wasn't going to agree to torture him. If the police hadn't arrived, do you think he'd have agreed to dump him with the car?"

"Conscience against self-preservation. It might have been a close thing. I'm glad we didn't have to find out the answer to that one."

McMurtrie was sleeping badly. He was dreaming. It was not always the same dream, but it always ended the same way, in a hopeless struggle, and a black and choking horror out of which he could only jerk himself by a convulsive physical effort.

The first time he did this he gave a scream which startled Sacher and Joscelyne out of sleep. By the third night they had got used to it, but it still worried them. Oddly, it did not occur to them to say anything to Mr. Fairfax; but Jared got permission to telephone his father, and as a result of what he said Ben Sacher canceled two important engagements and drove down to the school.

He walked for an hour with McMurtrie, over the soft grass and under the ancient trees, and as they walked, he talked. Afterward, McMurtrie was not able to remember all that was said between them, but he was conscious of the strength of the small, brown-faced man. It was a strength that he seemed able to pass on to his listener. When McMurtrie said, "How *could* he ever have done it?" Sacher said, "You mean, because he was a decent chap. That's the correct description, isn't it? I'm not laughing at you. That's what most people *would* have called Warr. He was not a strong character. Better men than him have given up more for the woman they wanted. Fortunes, careers, a kingdom even."

When they got tired of walking, they sat with their backs propped against the nabob's stone summerhouse. Sacher said, "There's violence everywhere in the world. It's increasing and it will go on increasing. Nobody who is young today can expect to go through his whole life without meeting violence. By coincidence you have run up against it twice in the last few months. It could be useful, or it could be harmful. That depends on you."

McMurtrie stretched out his legs and said, dreamily, "How do you mean?"

It was a novel but an oddly comforting thought, that the experience of violence might be useful. Like inoculation or having your tonsils out.

"I mean," said Ben Sacher, "that it has shown you a useful truth. That a man who is weak is easily corrupted, and being corruptible can be more dangerous than a stronger man. A bespectacled chicken farmer, when chance put power into his hands, murdered three million people and thought no more of it than eating his breakfast. But that's only one side of the lesson. You mustn't allow it to influence you too far in the other direction. Because you have looked inside an apparently agreeable man and found him hollow and black and vicious, you mustn't let this lead you into an automatic distrust of your fellow men. That would make you intolerably sour and cynical. No one is permitted to be cynical before he reaches the age of sixty."

McMurtrie grinned, and promised that he would do his best not to be cynical; for the next forty-six years at least.

After that visit he slept a great deal better.

Manifold walked down to the open-air stage between Colonel Brabazon and Sir Charles McMurtrie. The colonel said, "Your boy seems to have recovered his spirits. No permanent harm, I should say."

"They've got a natural resilience at that age," said Sir Charles.

"I hope to heaven you're right," said Manifold.

"Why do you say that?"

"If there were any permanent ill effects—I don't think there will be, but *if* there were—I don't think I should ever forgive myself."

"My dear fellow," said Colonel Brabazon, "it wasn't your fault."

"If I'd seen what was in front of my eyes it would never have happened."

"It's easy to be wise after the event," said Sir Charles.

Ahead of them Mr. Fairfax was talking to Mrs. Warlock. She said, "Billy tells me that Mr. Warr is in hospital."

"That's right. It was very sudden. A breakdown."

"You are having a lot of bad luck. First Mr. Mollison, then Mr. Warr."

"Ah, but Mollison's quite recovered. I had a letter from him this morning. He'll be rejoining us in September."

"That's a blessing, anyway. I'm told he was very popular with the boys. There's my husband waving."

Peter Warlock was in the front row, talking to the Paxtons. He said, "I had to move heaven and earth to get them to swap a matinee and an evening performance so that I could be here. I hope it's going to be worth it."

Mr. Paxton said, "Fine night. Shakespeare in the open. Acted by intelligent boys. Couldn't miss," and Mrs. Paxton said, "Of course it'll be lovely. Terence says they've been working terribly hard at it. They've hardly thought of anything else since half term."

"Quiet," said Mr. Paxton. "They're under starter's orders."

Feste, the clown, is usually thought of as thin, pale and melancholy. It had been a calculated risk to give the part to Monty Gedge, who was none of these things. His father watched him with anxious affection. Monty was all that was left to him of his stout-hearted little wife, who had died six years before. He realized, before the end of the play, that his son was going to be the success of the evening. Being a solemn boy, he spoke his lines in an offhand way that was more effective than any conscious effort to be funny, and he sang his songs in a small, cracked voice, hovering between treble and bass.

> "When that I was and a little tiny boy,
>   With hey, ho, the wind and the rain,
>   A foolish thing was but a toy,
>   For the rain it raineth every day."

Mr. Gedge was glad that it was dark, because there were tears in his eyes.

> "But when I came to man's estate,
>   With hey, ho, the wind and the rain,
>   'Gainst knaves and thieves men shut their gate . . ."

If only you could do it, thought Manifold. Lock the gate. Shut out all the disturbing influences, and live forever in an innocent cloud-cuckoo land among people who never grew up.

"A great while ago the world begun,
  With hey, ho, the wind and the rain;
  But that's all one, our play is done,
  And we'll strive to please you every day."